105 Steps

Steve Trigwell

Because of the dynamic nature of the internet, any web addresses or links contained in this book may have changed since publication and may no longer be valid. The views expressed in this book are solely those of the author and do not necessarily reflect the wider views of persons or persons referred to in links or web addresses contained herein.

ISBN: softcover   978-0-9752185-1-8

eBook   978-0-9752185-2-5

Copyright: © Stephen Trigwell 2021. All rights reserved. No part of this book may be used or reproduced by any means, audio- visual, motion picture, graphic, pictorial, electronic or mechanical, including photocopying, recording, taping or any information storage system without the written permission of the publisher.

Publisher: Stephen Trigwell

PO Box 1013, Bunbury 6231, Western Australia.

www.stephentrigwell.com

A catalogue record for this book is available from the National Library of Australia

Dedication

For my wife Glen, a loving, caring, amazingly inspirational woman. This story is incomplete, told through my eyes only. The real story belongs to her, my book is simply a gift of time. I look forward to piecing together our jigsaw life and spending the rest of my days by her side. My words shouldn't detract from her nightmare journey, locked away, untold until ready.

Table of Contents

Normal 1

Helter Skelter 9

Roller Coaster 25

Leap of Faith 39

Money, it's a Gas 53

Déjà Vu 67

Run Steve, Run 77

Marry Your Best Friend 99

The Dream 111

No Escaping Change 127

Back to the Future 135

A Great Sadness 145

The Beginning of the End 155

At Last the Golden Years 173

Unexpected Inspiration 195

Dream or Nightmare 203

Epilogue 211

Acknowledgment 223

Imagine yourself standing before a wide, deep, dark river. It's night time but, for some unknown reason, you know you must cross the river. You are alone and afraid. A large, white stepping stone slowly rises from the deep and you step out. It's firm and solid. Another white stepping stone appears in front of you. It too, is firm and solid. You take it. Then another, and another and another. The river is wide but your path is now long. You turn around to see how far you've come. There are no stones. There is only one stone, the one you are standing on.

This is a love story.

It's also a life story.

Normal

In one of his last ever movie scenes, Peter Sellers plays the innocent Chauncey Gardner in Being There. In his wonderful naivety, Chauncey wanders from a solemn graveside ceremony. Oblivious to the grief and despair, he nonchalantly strolls out across the surface of a lake. It's a beautiful scene where we are asked to question what reality really is.

I want to be Chauncey Gardner. I want to choose a reality where my wife Glen emerges from a nightmare of uncertainty and fear, despair and even death, to a place we all take for granted. What is normal? Is it waking up in the morning? Is it being able to speak? Eat? Think, drink, laugh, shit, wee, breathe, take a shower? Only when these things are taken away, do we truly appreciate "normal". I thought I understood my reality. Once upon a time, my normal was simply documenting Glen's daily medications after a stent was inserted into the right carotid artery, inside her head. I began writing a diary, a monotonous, boring record of her prescription drug taking as she recovered from lifesaving brain surgery. I never intended to write a book. For 26 days I diligently recorded each tablet until, on the 13th May 2021, our Humpty Dumpty fell off the wall. This story is about all the king's horses and all the king's men and women, trying to put Humpty back together again. Victims of modern society, with shortened attention spans, should jump to May 13th, I won't be offended.

Sat 17th April 2021

At last we are home. Arrived in Bunbury about 2.30pm. Dinner 7pm. I can't believe this nightmare is over. Karlee has draped a 'welcome home' banner on the kitchen wall and balloons are tied to the stairwell handrail. I write some words in a card ... "For my beautiful wife - the depth of your love never ceases to amaze me. Once again, I am in awe of your strength. This mountain cast a long, dark shadow but in your blindness, you somehow found a way. It doesn't seem fair that your gift of love should come at such a cost, but who are we to question? So long as you are never lost".

Glen took medications 7.10pm. Pain is in right temporal area, she doesn't recall that particular area being sore before. Very tender to touch. When she runs her finger over the skin she can't feel it, but when she applies pressure there it hurts. Pain = 7. No Endone at 7.10pm, maybe later if pain persists? Pain getting worse. Took Endone 8.30pm. Good sleep from 9 - 4.30am. Took 2 Panadol then back to sleep until 6.40am.

Sun 18th April

After waking and shower, a "different" sort of pain has begun on inside right of nose. The same tenderness to touch as with the still existing temporal pain. Pain = 6. At 1.30pm after lunch, a stabbing pain rated at 7 behind the right eye. Took 2 Panadol. Took all other meds at 7pm except Endone. 9.08pm pain constant, radiating into top of head, scale at a serious 8. Took an Endone now before bed. BP measured at 147/90. Pulse is 98. Glen eventually got to sleep at 11pm then woke at 2.30am. Took 2 Panadol, pain was about a 6. Fell asleep.

Mon 19th April

Woke about 6.30am, pain about 4-5. Took meds at 7.30am. Looked after little Addi for about 1hr, walked her to the beach. Went out for lunch with Maureen and Riley, came home slept for 1 hr and then went to Doctor Afolabi. Pain = 4. Had dinner at 5pm. Fell asleep again for 2 hrs woke at 7.30pm took meds. Had an Endone at 9.30pm. Watched TV then went to bed at 11.30pm, pain about 4-5. Rubbed cannabis oil, slept until 3.30am then took 2 Panadol.

Tues 20th April

Woke 6.50am. Pain about a 3-4 "not as bad as usual". Meds at 7.30am. Phill and Jude, Kimmie, Janet, Judy, Addi/Karlee/Dylan all visit. Missed Panadol at 2pm. No arvo sleep. Took 2 Panadol at 7pm. Lasagne and salad at 7pm. Meds at 7.30pm. Pain quite intense at 8pm rated at 6. Took an Endone at 8.45pm. Hit sack at 9.45pm pain rated at 5 but random sharp stabbing to 8. Rubbed cannabis oil topically. Woke up at 4.40am with pain at 3 (that's good) took 2 Panadol.

Wed 21st April

Woke again at 6.47am pain at 1. Overall headache present but no "pain" as it has been. Woke up after sleeping flat on back with just one pillow. Bit more pain upon standing up. Meds at 7.30am after Weetbix. 8.55am pain at 4. Midday stabbing pain reminded her she had missed taking Panadol at 10am - took 2 Panadol at 12 noon. Took another 2 x Panadol at 5.30pm. Took all other meds at 7.30pm. By 9.30pm pain rated at 4. Decided to take 2 x Panadol before going to bed at 10pm (rather than staying awake until 11.30 and taking an Endone before sleep) - did not take Endone before bed.

Thurs 22nd April

Woke at 5.20am. Good sleep, pain rating 2. Took 2 x Panadol at 5.20am. Had two poached eggs on toast. Took meds at 8.30am (one hour late, did not take Tapentadol trying to eliminate). At 9.50am intense pain on top of head (rated 8) and felt very nauseous, took the Tapentadol 9.54am. Took 2 Panadol at 11am. Had sleep in arvo 1.5 hrs. Took 2 Panadol at 5pm, another 2 Panadol at 10.15pm then bed. Good sleep until 5am then dozed until 7.20am.

Fri 23rd April

2 x Panadol at 5am (pain 2-3). Waking pain 7.20am score = 2. Meds at 7.30am. Visited Janet Roddy, rheumatoid arthritis specialist, at 8.30am. 2 x Panadol at 11am. Took another 25 mg Lyrica at 2pm (pain rated at 6), 2 x Panadol at 5pm, 2 x Panadol at 11pm. No Endone all day Going to sleep at midnight.

Sat 24th April

Woke at 5am took 2 Panadol went back to sleep woke again at 7am. Took meds 7.30am. Upped Lyrica to 50mg morning plus 50mg at night as per Janet Roddy. 2 x Panadol at 6 hr intervals all day as normal. Pain rating all day 2-3. Dinner at VAT restaurant, in bed by 10pm. Slept thru until 5am took 2 Panadol then back to sleep.

Sun 25th April

Woke at 7am. Pain rated 2-3. Trying to take just 2 x Panadol every 6 hrs with no Tapentadol and 50mg Lyrica twice a day. Seems to be keeping pain at 2-3 and more comfortable. Went to bed at 10pm. Woke at 4.30am took 2 x Panadol then sleep.

Mon 26th April

Woke at 7am pain rated at 2. Meds at 7.30am - now regularly taking the increased Lyrica as suggested by Janet Roddy (50mg twice a day). Panadol x 2 every 6 hrs. Still getting occasional stabbing pain but less intensity and "bearable". Pain about 2.

Tues 27th April

Ditto as per yesterday ... except at 6pm pain was about 4.

Wed 28th April

Ditto but 50mg Lyrica morning ... 75mg at night. Had good day all day. Pain 2.

Thurs 29th April

Normal meds morning includes 2mg Prednisolone, trying 75mg Lyrica in morning. Travelled to Balingup to get wedding ring redesigned, at about 10.40am pain increased on top of head? headache, pain in eye socket, altered sensation in hands, fingers feel a bit tingly, pins and needles hands and feet, feeling a bit weak, funny. Also, at 10.43am altered sensation on right side palette, top of roof of mouth. Had an early lunch, felt a bit better after food. Panadol as per normal every 6 hrs x 2. Did not take Tapentadol in evening, normal meds.

Fri 30th April

Panadol 2 tabs every 6 hrs (incl. usually say 2-3am morning). Not taking any more Tapentadol. Still took 75mg Lyrica in morning plus std. 2 mg Prednisolone. 75mg Lyrica again at night. Pain rating at 10pm = 4. Due for Panadol now. Took 2.

Sat 1st May

Woke at 5am took 2 Panadol. Pain at 5.49am is ~3. 75mg Lyrica morning and night, Panadol x 2 every 6 hrs. Normal 2mgs Prednisolone and RA drugs. Haven't taken any Tapentadol or Endone since last mentions. Sleeping well. Rubbing cannabis oil on temple region and 2 drops under tongue (only at night). Basically, only painkillers taken are Lyrica and Panadol.

Sun 2nd May

As per yesterday. Pain rating has subsided to a relative constant ~2. Has noticed occasional stabbing pains are usually due to movement- i.e. gravity when bending down, looking up etc. 8.55pm after Pam Bilsby visit, left eye is a bit painful - described as "clamping up"? very strange, very uncomfortable pain, rating 5. Weird tightness like "sucking it in"? or something - maybe nerves? Bit more painful than it has been recently.

Mon 3rd May

Plan from now on is Panadol (2) every 6 hrs and Lyrica (75mg) morning and night. Blood thinners as per normal Ticagrelor half a tablet morning and night. Aspirin 1 tablet daily, plus rheumatoid arthritis drugs methotrexate/Prednisolone/folic/Humira/vitamin D.

Tues 4th May

Drugs ditto as to Monday 3rd. Pain rating as a general (all day) up and down between 2-5. Left Glen at home and I painted caravan.

Wed 5th May

Drugs ditto ... pain rating better, generally about a 2 all day - bit worse in evening getting tired - sewing /concentrating.

Thurs 6th May

All going well, no real change, meds same. Pain rating 2-3. Maybe some feeling returning to top/back of scalp?

Fri 7th May

Same, same. Morning pain rated at 3. Maybe some feeling coming back to the top right eyelid. Sensing the "lower third" of the top eyelid on right side. Feeling coming back?

Sat 8th May

Good sleep. Pain rating ~2. By 10pm some stabbing pains behind eye/due for Panadol now.

Sun 9th May

No real change

Mon 10th May

Managed with 2 doses of Panadol - 5am and again at 9pm. Felt good all day. Pain rating 2.

Tues 11th May

Same as yesterday ... but some sharper stabbing pains 10pm. Still only 2 x Panadol 6am and 10.30pm. 75mg Lyrica morning and night as per every day now including yesterday. Pain 2.

Wed 12th May

Ditto. Drove to Perth. Lunch with Johnny Luscombe. Scan tomorrow.

Stephen Trigwell

Helter Skelter

Thurs 13th May

Worst day of our life. Scan 6.30am ... news not good. Aneurysm grown from 25mm to 33mm. I send a text to my mate Mick: "Mate the scan was not good. We were expecting the aneurysm to shrink but in fact it has grown from 25mm to 33mm. Neuro surgeon was surprised and obviously disappointed, open brain surgery not an option ... so after a team meeting they have decided best option is to immediately stop blood thinners. Suspect aneurysm growing thru capillary feed in walls of aneurysm - highly unusual. Been there for a long time apparently. After stopping thinners, plan is aneurysm then fully clots, stops growing and eventually shrinks. Risk of stroke is high within next week or so (in particular), then diminishes somewhat after that (don't ask me how). Shit scenario ... but it is what it is. Glen a bit shocked and still processing it all ... might just take a week off mate. We are staying at Hannah's tonight and tomorrow - then booking into Cottesloe for a week. Glen wants to see the beach"

Fri 14th May

Staying at Hannah's. Dylan took day off work, Jake flying home from Roy Hill. We're all in a bit of shock. No blood thinners. This is fucked.

Sat 15th May

Jake flew in 6pm last night. Glen was very tired yesterday. 2 hrs sleep in arvo then fairly good sleep overnight. Bit of a headache in morning. Booked in to 11 Warnham Street Cottesloe with family until Fri 21st May.

Sun 16th May

Received a phone call from Sir Charles Gairdner Hospital (SCGH). Glen to go immediately for admission - meeting tomorrow morning with Professor Lind and all family members, regarding plan for surgery Tuesday with team of neuro surgeons. Find out more tomorrow. Hannah sends an email to Charlie Teo, a Sydney brain surgeon well known for successfully taking on difficult cases. I do an online search for Professor Christopher Lind, I'm satisfied we undoubtedly have the best guy in Australasia looking at Glen.

Mon 17th May

Shitting ourselves. Professor Lind proposes a surgical solution whereby they take a vein from her left forearm and bypass the aneurysm with a new blood flow to the right side of her brain. We all sit stunned. He is telling us Glen is a walking time bomb, at imminent risk of a massive stroke or brain death. He says the op is "not a walk in the park". Glen decides do it, on the proviso that if she turns out "a vegetable" we switch her off. How do we define vegetable? Who switches her off? Dylan says he's selfish and doesn't want to lose her. I send Mick a text:

"This is the guy we saw this morning.

https://www.sjog.org.au/find-a-specialist/search-results/l/i/n/d/lind-christopher-raymond-peter

Scheduled op tomorrow 7-8am start ... all day op. Possibly sedated for at least 24hrs post op. Risks = 10% disaster, 90% success. Risk nevertheless. Risk of stroke/death if do nothing = 50% and increasing in time. We're feeling positive"

Tues 18th May

Met Glen at hospital. Ward 66 Room 4D. At 6am walked to green lifts, met all the kids. Back to Glen's room, bit of a delay while waiting for transfer off to theatre at ~7am. Prof Lind has told us it will be an "all day op". Took kids to zoo then we all waited in Cottesloe. Hell of a day. Gets worse as day goes on. Everybody is tense ... no news, we rang SCGH at 7.04pm - Glen still in operating theatre. At 9.53pm we received a call from an unknown number. It's Professor Lind to say op just finished - all good it went well. Everyone in tears of joy. What a relief. That guy is a fucking genius - what a guy! Glen under sedation for the next 12 hours at least. Going into intensive care unit (ICU) now. 3 kids, Kade and I sit around sharing the relief. Some humour, a few beers and a glass of port, joking in awe of the expertise of Lind, absolute awe and respect. He said aneurysm should begin to shrink within "hours and days" ... we all laugh as Jake misheard him to say "a thousand days?" Lind comes across as such a pro, his delivery so calm, measured and reassuring. We're told Glen will be heavily sedated for at least 12 hrs so will try and get some sleep before heading in 6am tomorrow. Not out of woods yet. Thank you, God. Simple as that.

Wed 19th May

Set alarm for 5.00am. Woke at 4.55am. Blocked alarm and had a shower, leaving ASAP for hospital, left phone on vol last night - no news is good news. In ICU there is a nurse at her bedside 24/7, gotta go. New day time nurses are Sam and Courtney. I noticed last blood pressure (BP) reading was 107/94, then another at 102/63. At 7.30am Sam just told me they are going to give her some fluid to try and get that up a bit. Sent Glen for CT scan ~9.30am, spoke to Sam at 10.50pm, radiologist, doctors etc. will discuss findings and work plan for going forward. Signs appear stable but some weakness evident on left side of body. Scans possibly showing low blood flow on top of head, could be low BP, this is what they are discussing apparently.

ICU Doctor Dorian asked Dylan, Jake and me in for a private discussion. Ominous little room. He told us after the 3 scans they did, plus the weakness in the left side - that surgeons would have to go in again, immediately, and re do the entire arterial bypass, this time using a vein from Glen's right leg. I don't believe it. Apparently not enough blood passing thru to a certain area of the brain. Risk of stroke is now elevated even more but again, the risk of doing nothing is catastrophic. Prof Lind will do the op again. They are confident they can do it, but have explained the increased risks. I don't do "negative" so, for myself and my family, and everyone I know, my mind will not entertain an unfavourable outcome. She is a wonderful fighter, we all whispered in her ear and I know she heard us. They wheeled Glen into theatre again at 12.30pm. Friends have been texting me constantly, asking about Glen so I'm just sending a group text update. Everyone is as stunned as we are. This is when I sit on the beach and ask one more time, for all the prayers, all the energy, all the wishes ... even the casual thoughts. I text:

"I'm so sorry to do this to you all as I know we ALL have worries etc in our lives ... but I can only help assemble a force powerful enough to do this with the love of every person Glen and I know. It's why I text like I do. This is the big stage, Glen can do this with all our help. Sorry to lob it on you, but even if you don't believe, please spare a thought/prayer for Glen. She'll be in theatre all day, again, and we won't hear for a long time. Stay with me, I will text when it becomes appropriate".

It's 2.39pm ... she's fighting like fuck. I know it, I can see her through these tears. Go you good thing go! I'm on the beach. Luscombe rings, he "just happens" to be in Cottesloe. I meet him. Mick comes down. My best man and my groomsman from 1982, I couldn't have picked two better blokes. We share a couple of beers and I shed a couple of tears. I'm trying to hold myself together but I'm a fucking mess. Back to the house, Dylan cooks a BBQ. We're all trying to deal with it, few words are spoken. I play some soft guitar, as we have each done over the past few days. We wait. I fall asleep on the bed. 11.16pm we get another call from the unknown number, Prof Lind. It's not the news we want to hear. The second bypass has failed. He says the vein looked good, they were meticulous, the op went well, they kept Glen in the operating theatre for an hour watching the bypass pumping blood, then slowly, it began to turn a "dusky pink" as it clotted. We talk about reasons, it's quite technical and there are several but, in the end, it doesn't matter. It didn't work. I take a shower. Hannah drives me to the hospital. Dylan and Jake take another car. We need to whisper in her ear, tell her we love her and everything will be alright. We all comfort Glen, I stay to hold her hand, falling asleep at her bedside. ICU nurse Jane turns Glen at 3.15am and asks me if I intend staying, I mention Hannah was going to swap with me. Jane says maybe better to leave it until say 6am, as they need to wash her and "do a few things". I decide to drive back to Cottesloe. Spoke to Hannah when I got back, she can't sleep. I lay down at 4.03am, empty.

Thurs 20th May

Woke at 7am Hannah and Jake already in ICU. Dylan and I head over, no change with Glen. I read the ICU nurses day sheet - sedation Propofol was set at 20 early morning, hourly recordings from ~9.30am they started halving it, by 10.30 it's 10, by 11.30 it's 5, by 12.30 it's 1 ... and by 1.30pm sedation is off. From now on we are hoping for some response. I'm grasping at straws here, very occasional right arm movement. At ~2pm the ICU Doctor comes, new hi flow vein bypass definitely not working, already some brain damage. Too early to tell but still expecting her to awaken, just maybe not today. There is swelling of the brain and some known infarcted or dead brain cells. They are predicting a high likelihood of no left arm and impaired left leg function, but hard to know how serious leg will be, "not out of the woods yet". He is saying sensation and motor function are separate. Glen is not moving. I'm crying, sobbing. I get another call from the unknown number, a phone call from neuro surgeon Doctor Raj. He and Prof Lind want to see me at 6pm for a talk. I ring Hannah, Dylan and Jake individually, as I drive to the hospital. This will be in the ominous interview room. I am dreading this conversation. Please help me God. I go to the toilet near the green lifts. When I re-enter the ICU, I see the other patients sitting, talking, smiling, laughing on the phone, and I'm thinking why can't my wife be like that? Why can't I just turn the corner and there she is, sitting up, joking, laughing, smiling. It's just terrible to see her like this. I know Glen so well - I am truly dreading this conversation with Lind. I hope Hannah gets here in time. We're in the room before the doctors. We've all said our piece, but we are all so selfish, we don't want her to go. Each of us, in our way want to keep her for our own reasons. Jake and Dylan for unborn babies, all 3 because they love their Mum and have never known life without her. Me? Because she's my soul mate, my life partner, my other half, my duo team member. I can't imagine life without her.

The meeting: I audio record the entire meeting with Prof Lind's permission. Raj and Lind together. Lind describes how the bypass operation involved a low flow and a high flow bypass. The low flow involved stitching the right side superficial temporal artery onto a small branch of the middle cerebral artery, one of the main arteries of the brain supplied by the carotid. The idea behind the low flow, is to provide a small flow of blood to the carotid area from the side, while the carotid is clipped during the high flow bypass. The radial artery from Glen's left arm was then stitched into the internal carotid artery in Glen's neck, for the high flow bypass. Once the high flow graft was complete, clips were placed on the carotid artery isolating the aneurysm. The low flow from the first bypass op was a success and is functioning well, carrying more blood than before, however as we knew, the high flow failed. A second, high flow bypass was immediately performed, using a vein from the right leg, "it looked really good, a lot better than the original we thought, then watching it in real time it gradually went dusky as we watched a prothrombotic cascade through the whole vein, it was so diffuse we couldn't salvage it". In some positive news, he explains how it's possible for the low flow vein diameter to sometimes double in size from 1.5mm over months, based on angiograms.

Lind says "we are not feeling nihilistic, we are not completely despondent, we've seen people rehabilitate very well from similar scans, all is not lost". When Hannah suggests "it's not unrealistic to expect things can improve", Lind answers "not at all". After the meeting we are feeling so much more positive. I cannot overstate how relieved we all are after his prognosis. We now also realise our expectation of stimulus response time was probably way too narrow as well. Lind is confident that "every shift where she is stable with no problems, is a win".

As we wait outside ICU before leaving, Rodger arrives at the ICU waiting area to see us. Rodger is Mum's favourite nurse from High Dependency Unit (HDU). He is such a caring man. He looked after her after the first stent op on March 26th, before Easter. He came all the way down from another ward level in his break, just to comfort us and enquire about Glen. Rodger is a gentle man and says he is looking forward to caring for her in HDU after ICU. We all go home for sleep except Dylan. Dyl stays with his Mum, slight increase in movements, coughing and right arm movement attempting to pull the ventilator out. About 9.30pm Jake takes over, Dyl stays for a while. Doctor says we need to run some tests and suggests both wait in waiting room. When they go back in, the nurse advises them she is quite responsive at the moment. During the tests Glen had her hand to her face almost trying to extricate the ventilator. Dyl leaves at 9.45pm. Jake stays and sees Glen reaching to rip out the ventilator a couple of times. Glen also physically showing discomfort when nurse sucking excess fluid from her mouth. Doctors suggest Jake go home, again politely not wanting any other family members to take over the night shift. Dylan wakes me when Jake returns with the news of Glen's movements, it's a bit distressing for me to imagine but we all agree it's a step in the right direction. With some light at the end of the tunnel we escape with some bad humour.

Jake - "I asked Mum who her favourite son was and she pointed to me".

"Yeah, that's when she pointed alright, but her first word was … Dylan!"

We laugh about how distraught we were pre-meeting, how we were pleading with Glen to move, yelling, begging God for help. Crying out for some sign, how I even took the guitar into ICU and sang a song. About how we saw BP changes when we urged her on and goaded her to climb Kilimanjaro. Then we recall Prof. Lind softly saying at our meeting, "our immediate goal now is just to keep her very calm and stable". We feel like we were doing the opposite.

Poor Mum. Poor Glen. She is such a fucking fighter. We all saw her try so hard to move her arm when we pleaded. Just to make us happy. We should have left her in her "stable state". I decide not to go to hospital for shift change. I will leave these wonderful health professionals to care for my baby, my beautiful lady, my team member, my life partner. My understanding of love has gone up another level. I now think I have an inkling of what Glen has always known. Her instincts in times like this have always astounded me, she is everything that I am not. The reverse can probably equally be said of me. When I see the stars, she sees the whole of the moon. That's why I know we make such an amazing team together. I very rarely go to Church, but all who know me know that I have been talking and working with my God for many years now. I consider us friends. I trust Him. I only say "Him", because a smart guy once said "Our Father". When I was a little boy, I grew up with stories of The Great War and The Second World War. There was a saying I remember, "there are no atheists in the trenches". I know that trench well.

Fri 21st May

4.58am I awaken and immediately shower, dress and pack as we must be out of the accommodation by 10am. I want to get to ICU early but not too early. After last night's news of more movement I am a little anxious about seeing Glen in distress with the ventilator. Maybe she's improved enough for the team to take it out? Will her eyes be open? Or is that too much, too quick to ask? I'm trying not to get ahead of myself. It's hard. I had a good sleep. It's still dark as I drive past the red and blue flashing neon light - Fish and Chips, Ice Cream, Fish and Chips, Ice Cream. I'm filled with apprehension on the drive, how will she be? I'm so wanting to be able to take a photo of her sitting up smiling, waving, so I can send it to the kids.

Hannah, Dylan and Jake usually take the gold lifts to 4th floor. I always take the green lifts. Left into the short corridor then right into the long corridor, another right then left to ICU. I pick up the handset and they let me in. She's asleep, calm. Part of me is relieved to see her peaceful, another part fades with the disappointment of over expectation. No smile, no sitting up, no laugh. I whisper in her ear that I am there but she seems to be sleeping, after listening to Lind yesterday I am happy with that. I overhear the nurse changeover conversation, it sounds like Glen had a stable night.

I think of my mate, poor "Doc" Stewart. I met Stewie in Africa, in 1974. His wife Dot is in ICU in Hollywood Hospital, about a kilometre from here. I know he is sitting by her bed just like I am. I say a prayer for them both. ICU Doctor comes and examines Glen for signs of response. I'm not sure it's brilliant. He calls for her to wake up, open her eyes ... no response. He speaks of the arm movement being localised instead of "withdrawn" or reflexive, the nurse tells me that is good, it means Glen is purposefully moving her right arm. In this test her right leg movement is not pronounced, even slight withdrawal, but nurse Brooke tells me it's not really an issue yet, can be better understood when she wakes up. Doctor orders another CT scan sometime today. Lind spoke of a known "bleed" in her brain which he said wasn't a concern "yet" but if this bleed gets any worse they will have to operate again to relieve. This CT scan will show it. I'm getting so many text messages of support, we can do this. The level of care here is relentless, I can feel the dedication. The new day nurse Brooke continually busies herself - mouth swabs, checking pupils, checking data feeds, recording, talking to Glen the whole time, apologising for inconvenience. They turn the overhead lights on.

Hannah arrives, she is a wonderful rock of support. As she speaks to her Mum, I know Glen would be so proud of her. Hannah quizzes the nurse. Some of this stuff goes straight past a 67-year-old bloke, but I know if it's important Hannah will fill us all in. Brooke is still purposefully busy tidying, changing IV bags, twisting, fiddling with tubes, taking blood samples. Hannah has prepared a text:

"I'm here and Mum's doing good, no real change. The ICP (intra cranial pressure) went up to 20 last body roll, so they have started a new drug via infusion to help remove excess fluid from brain. It had already reduced to 10 when I came back in, so nothing to be concerned about at the moment. Just a preventative precaution to ensure it doesn't stay elevated for long periods of time. Come back whenever you like I'll stay a while longer xx".

Hannah explains to me that Glen's brain pressure has gone up a little and her oxygen levels have decreased a bit. I think this is a bit alarming but the nurse assures me its ok, and Hannah says so long as it's not elevated for long periods of time it should be ok. The pressure could be up because of the bleed, this is why they are sending her for the scan this morning. I send Hannah our Spotify playlist and she plays it thru her phone to Glen. Glen moves her right arm a little. Maybe she doesn't like Michael Buble? Then it's Elvis ... she loves Elvis.

Brooke is the butt of ICU jokes because she dyed her hair blonde. It's nice to hear all the nurses laugh, the morale seems good. She keeps working, pushing "stuff" into the nasogastric tube - I guess this is food? She checks the tubes coming from Glen's groin area, so many tubes ... pushes more "stuff" through. Stevie Wonder - Superstition. Glen tries to cough, it's awkward, Brooke is onto it before it happens and suctions out any fluid. She cleans the tube with a disposable flush fluid, then gently wipes Glen's eyes clean. Dean Martin - Volare (Glen loves Dean Martin). I'm crying now. Aretha Franklin - R.E.S.P.E.C.T, Sam Cooke - Dock of the Bay, Etta James - At Last.

Wearing glasses and a pink hair clasp, Brooke is constantly working, now checking and changing drainage bags, stethoscope checking chest, heart, opens a foolscap file and hand writes data. She sanitizers her hands. One of Glen's favourite dance songs comes on - Robin Thicke and Pharrell Williams. I remember the time we rented a houseboat with some friends and partied all night to Blurred Lines. Glen had insisted the girls dress in zebra striped onesies and, after 4 or 5 bottles of red and Disco Inferno by The Trammps, we out-partied the other house boat pulled up on the adjacent mooring. The CT scan is scheduled for about 10am. We are hoping the bleed has either stopped or not progressed. Brooke wheels out the oxygen bottle for replacement, this girl is a machine. 9.18am they arrive to take Glen for the scan. Hannah tells me this scan is important because it will determine whether the brain bleed has stopped, slowed or gotten worse. Glen's head pressure has gone up from ~2 to 6-7, we are hoping it's just the 3rd day peak of swelling Prof Lind spoke of. We both go back to Cottesloe to help with checking out from the accommodation, then Hannah goes for a swim. I suggest I'll visit Stewie but Jake and Hannah reckon I should relax with the family. Tegan heads back to Margaret River. Jake has found his soulmate for sure. The rest of us sit on the beach at Cottesloe, as usual I'm the only one who doesn't swim. The kids all head back to

Hannah's house and I text Stewie, as I figure I could quickly visit him (and maybe Dot) to give him some support, but he's waiting on a meeting with Dot's oncologist - I know exactly what that poor bastard is going thru. Sorry Stewie.

I drive to Claremont Quarter so I can park the car before ringing Rick Thomas, the Balingup Goldsmith. Glen had put a ring in to be re-made, with diamonds and white gold to match the new one I had recently bought her. I'd love to have the new ring ready to give her when she wakes up. If it's ready, I'd make a flash trip down to collect it. I explain the circumstances to Rick and he asks how has she recovered from the op? I break down on the phone with her image in my head. The diamonds haven't arrived. I pretend to shop thru MJ Bale thinking I need a new shirt, but I know I only ever want to look good for her, and I don't really need a new shirt anyway. I'll head back to the hospital.

12.34pm I take the green lifts again to 4th floor. Out of the lift, left then right again down the long corridor and around the bend to ICU. 105 steps. Dylan is already there. No scan results yet. Inter Cranial Pressure (ICP) back down to 2/3, Blood Pressure (BP) allowed in range of 110-140, it's sitting at 124-126 with no adrenaline. Brooke is all over it but at 1.14pm she is in changeover conversation with new shift nurse. I'll be sorry to see her go. I thank Brooke and the new nurse is Alicia. Being at Glen's bedside holding her hand feels so much better than pretending to shop at M J Bale. I'm holding her left foot and every now and again she lifts her big toe. I convince myself it's because I'm holding and stroking it, hope I'm right. Dylan questions Alicia about the scan today - we know today is the 3rd day from op and we were told max swelling is 3-5 days from op. They've told us the bleed is a tiny bit bigger but if Lind is concerned he will speak with us after scan review. ICP or head pressure, is apparently a general "all over" stat, not measuring a specific problem area, we'll wait on Lind. I lift the sheet from her foot because I know she doesn't like her feet to get too hot. Dylan places his lucky piece of sea glass on the back of her left hand. At 2.30pm Alicia asks us politely if we can leave while they move her in the bed, I always fear this is when they do some pain tolerance tests or something. We go downstairs for a while, in the sunshine. My brother Russell calls and wants to meet me for brekky on Sunday … "brings back memories" he says. I know he is thinking of his wife Fran, who died from cancer in 2001. I say I'll text him. He is probably going to the Dockers football game - he and Glen can go into rehab together. If anyone can rehab Russell into an Eagles supporter it'll be Glen.

I head back up and there's Rodger again, chatting with Dylan, asking about Glen. He's such a nice bloke. He loves fishing. When all this is over I might try to set him up on Luscy's boat for a short trip to the Abrolhos Islands. Glen not ready yet - Dylan and I both fall asleep momentarily in ICU waiting room. 3.30pm back in ICU with Glen. I tell her I'm back and straight away she moves her right arm. I tell her I love her and how beautiful she is and her mouth starts to construe and squirm. I just know she's in there. Alicia tells me she hasn't had a bowel movement in a while. I remember Glen went to the toilet moments before being wheeled out for the first op on May 18th - ever the nurse. They are going to give her a suppository and clean it up this afternoon. I think of the care they give, and I'm so proud of the long career Glen had as a registered nurse and midwife. As I'm tapping these words into my phone I imagine looking up and there she is just watching me with open eyes, but no. Hannah drives from Embleton to take over from Dylan watching Mum. She suggests I take the opportunity to drive to Micks place in Peppermint

Grove. He and his wife Tracey have kindly offered me a bed as Glen recovers. It's only a short drive from SCGH. I grab 2.5 hrs sleep and drive back to hospital after a short chat with Tracey. 12 years ago, Tracey faced her own long battle with cancer. She won. Mick was my best man when I married Glen on 14th August 1982, they are a great support for me in this. I head back to ICU, before Hannah and I are politely asked to leave at 10pm. When Glen was wheeled out after her first op, I was allowed to stay until 3.30am. Gradually as time has passed and she has stabilised a little, they are asking us to leave earlier. I'm taking this as a positive. I think if Glen was in dire peril they would let me stay. Back in Peppermint Grove, Mick is home and we chat about everything. I first met Mick in 1974. I had just flown 14 hrs in a "jumbo" 747 from Perth to Johannesburg, arriving 6th June with a backpack and a guitar. We became friends almost immediately before he travelled north to what was then Rhodesia, now Zimbabwe. I left Joburg and meandered my way south, eventually pausing in Port Elizabeth (PE), now re-named Gqeberha, where one night, dancing on a tabletop in a nightclub, I heard a voice yelling "Steve, Steve". I looked across and there was Mick and Stewie.

As I'm chatting with Mick, we watch the last half of the Brisbane Lions v Richmond AFL game from the Gabba in Brisbane. The Lions win it 102 to 74. We both agree Brisbane could well win the premiership this year. While watching the football I get a text from Stewie. "Hi Steve and Glen, Dot passed away at 8.35pm this evening. XG". We are both devastated. Of course, the timing of this tragedy is not lost on me and, in my mind, I resolve to double down on my positivity for Glen. I take a shower and hit the sack at midnight, sleeping well until my alarm goes off at 5.10am. I'll take the morning shift sitting with Glen.

Stephen Trigwell

Roller Coaster

Sat 22nd May

I'm in the hospital car park at 5.57am. This time it's only 95 steps from the green lifts to ICU. My resolve has increased but not doubled ... yet. I only have to get it down to 52.5 steps and I'm there! At this early hour, there is no receptionist at the little ICU window. I pick up the handset for a connection direct to the ward where the duty nurse tells me they are attending to some personal duties with Glen and "would I like a cup of tea while I wait?" I'm allowed in at 6.23am. Rebecca tells me she has been stable all night. First thing I notice is her head pressure is 18-20. Lind told us this level approaches concern however the nurse assured me Glen has just been rolled and moved. Rebecca suggests it's best not to touch or speak to Glen at the moment. Her face is swollen with fluid retention and I'm hoping this is not a reflection of what is going on in her brain. I sense this weekend will be tough as Glen pushes through this risky period post op. The ICP is hovering between 16-19/20 and her BP is 143/69. The ICP data alarm beeps at 21. I'm worried. Back to 17, 15, 17. Rebecca and another nurse are busying themselves around Glen ... checking tubes, measuring syringes, checking data feed. It's 6.45am. 138/65 and ICP 16. 6.57am Glen is motionless, BP 137/100 ICP slightly better at 15.

For the first time in ages I check my Twitter feed. I only ever use Twitter for stocks and crypto. The first post I see is from someone I don't know, asking about another handle I share common ideas and investment codes with. Apparently, he's unwell so I DM wishing him all the best, after that I decide I don't need to check Twitter anymore. Rebecca turns Glen's head slightly and almost immediately the ICU drops to 11-12 then dips to 10. I'm happier. Why didn't she do that before?

The new day nurse Tarah (not her real name) arrives for the changeover and they ask me to wait outside. I message Homer, I know he is a very good friend of Stewie. Homer was also in the Port Elizabeth nightclub the night I danced on the table. It was the same night Tom and I hot-wired a Mini from the underground car park to drive home. We were the last to leave the club and with no transport, Tom figured the Mini owner wouldn't mind if we borrowed it for a while. We never damaged the car, left the key in the ignition and parked it just up the road from where we lived, 1a Havelock Square in PE. It was there for a week before the cops came for it. I know Homer will wrap his arms around Stewie. Mick and Homer see a lot more of Stewie than I do as they all live in Perth. Glen and I live in Bunbury, 2 hrs away by car.

I'm allowed back in at 8.09am. First thing I notice is ICP back at 9 and BP is 131/60. I'm so relieved to see ICP coming down. As I text Hannah my observations and receive her medicalesq responses, it occurs to me we have a much bigger team at work here. I think of Mary, Janet, Judy, Pam and the legion of nursing friends Glen made over the years who are so eager to see her well again. We've got to get thru this. 8.30am - ICP 7 ... 9 ... 5 ... 6... 10, 8.40am - ICP 4 ... BP 142/73 As I'm typing and I notice the bed sheet moving. She's lifting her left and right toes a bit, as I look up she sort of squirms her shoulders. I'm happy with anything. She starts dribbling so I alert Tarah. ICP = 1 right now, Tarah sucks out excess mouth fluid ICP up to 3-4. Glen seems to be wriggling a little bit, not sure if it's purposeful or reflexive. ICP at 3. 8.56am ICP at 9, 10, 8, 7, 6, 5 BP 105/74 they reposition the BP tube and it goes to 130/66. 9.19am I'm not a nurse but to me it looks like Glen has slumped down the bed a bit, data is ok ICP 5, BP 130/69. I notice Glen is dribbling again, I don't want to interrupt Tarah's conversation with another nurse about her 5 days off in Rottnest so, I take a tissue and dab Glen's mouth dry. It feels good to do something to help. I feel so useless. Her skin is still tight from fluid retention. Tarah is the most aloof nurse Glen has had, sitting on other side of the room talking to a colleague about random social matters. Tarah is now down the far end of the ICU room laughing with another nurse. I know I'm a bit focussed but shit, this is my wife in ICU! I berate myself for being so judgemental. Without knowing, I reckon Tarah is a part timer - it's the weekend now. She's the opposite to young Brooke. I dab the dribble from Glen's mouth again and comment that she seems to have slumped in the bed. Tarah doesn't seem too worried. After the third time I dab the dribble, Tarah politely asks if I can step out for 20 minutes while they reposition Glen. I will be interested to see the ICP reading.

Allowed back in with boys at ~10.30am. Glen repositioned upon re-entry ICP about 17. Tarah tells us Glen is booked in for another scan this morning, according to Tarah yesterday's scan was "pretty bad". That's the first time we've heard that sort of description from anyone. While Tarah is still at the foot of the bed she tells us that the surgeons can go back in and remove bone/skull to relieve pressure - but in next breath tells us that the procedure can greatly increase the probability of further disabilities because of brain movements. Glen appears to be getting squirmy and sort of agitated so I cut Tarah off mid-sentence and say "ok that's enough Tarah, let's not have this conversation here in front of Glen". Glen's ICP is now 22, and her BP went to 180 before dropping to 160. I was so annoyed - that conversation shouldn't be had anywhere near Glen. I freak out a bit. I don't care what they say about how much can one understand/hear while unconscious. She's not on any sedatives for fucks sake! I reckon she heard that for sure. Glen and I had a conversation before she consented to the very first op and, I know her biggest fear was being left in a totally dependent state on life support. She told me she would rather go ... "switch me off" she said ... couldn't bear for her two granddaughters Marley and Addi to see her that way. No way Tarah should have had that conversation right there at her bedside. Her ICP was dropping again ~15 when we were asked to leave so they could prep her for the scan. We ask to speak to ICU Doctor on duty, can't see him until after scans come back.

11.09am we take the green lifts to ground ... walking out we run into Michael Wallis. Michael is a Consultant Hepatologist at SCGH and is a close personal friend of Hannah's. He has a patient in the bed opposite Glen in ICU. We had a half hour conversation with him, now feeling a lot better. He basically said don't pay too much attention to nurse's comments, wait on doctor's advice, nurse info can sometimes be opinionated and unreliable. He says another scan represents no danger and provides good data. He's happy to chat anytime. Feeling much better. I decide to use this time to get some clothes washed, then quickly dismiss that idea and duck to Claremont Quarter again - 2 x Tommy Hilfiger polos, Coles for some jocks and socks, then back to Mick's house.

Suddenly, I get a call from the unknown number, Doctor Oleg another ICU neuro surgeon. Glen's ICP is too high for too long.

He suggests an open brain operation called a decompression craniectomy. Fark! This feels like a disaster, when do we win a fucking trick here? I'm totally and utterly fucking devastated. Big risk of left (good) brain side damage if we don't do it. At the moment the left side is unaffected. If we don't do this op the risk of a massive stroke and even brain death elevates dramatically. A time bomb with a very short fuse. The op is on for this afternoon and Prof Lind has rescheduled to do it. Oleg wanted my consent - I gave it.

As I'm driving I call the kids, I've arranged an immediate ICU meeting with Doctor Oleg. It's raining steadily as I pull into the car park. The smell of petrichor hangs in the air and again, I think of Glen and the times we have discussed what a shit word "petrichor" is. For such a unique and evocative smell, we always agreed the word seemed so underwhelming. I'm sobbing. Surely, 51 years can't end like this, in a flash of nothingness. This time, it's only 64 steps from the green lifts to ICU. Hannah is already in with Glen. She's sobbing too. I ask her to step away from Glen momentarily, but she tells me she has already told Glen about the op. Hannah explains to me ... "Mum knows all about these procedures and she would want to know". We retreat to the ICU waiting room for a family meeting with Dylan and Jake.

We all decide that we have no real option. We are all on the same page. With no damage to left side of brain and no further damage from pressure if she can pull thru this, she may come out of this with a limp left arm and semi deficit left leg, plus a massive headache for months, more than likely full speech and right-side movement. I'll just have to clean her arse I guess! If she can just hold her grandchildren I know she'll be happy. Doctor Oleg tells me his name is actually Omar, "as in Omar Sharif". I ask if he is also Egyptian, like the great actor, "No I'm from Pakistan". I'm feeling anguish mixed with a weird sense of pride. Anguish about the op and Glen's critical state, but pride in this fantastic country we call our home. Sir Charles Gairdner Hospital is a microcosm of multicultural inclusiveness and equality, and I feel good that so many people from so many countries and so many walks of life have made this place their home. Many have either brought or learnt extraordinary skills. I'm grateful. The 4 of us have the meeting, no sugar coating. Doctor Omar (Sharif) says they take out a section of her skull the size of an adult palm, store it in a sterile environment for months if necessary, before replacing it. Dylan raises his concerns about the risks of three hourly turning and moving Glen after her skull has been removed. We are looking at months of rehabilitation and body mending but that's ok, I'm up for it. I just pray that she doesn't get any more brain damage. We sit in silence. Nothing more to say.

Glen goes in at 5pm. We stand around outside Block G wondering what to do, then Hannah suggests Mum would want us to stick together with a view of the ocean and to share a drink. We settle on the Cottesloe Hotel and resort to humour to break the tension as we wait. I threaten to blackmail my brother Gerry's wife Rosalie, into divulging her secret carrot cake recipe as motivation for Glen to survive and wake up. Dylan theorises the human brain is like Google maps constantly establishing new pathways ... very plausible. To quote Darryl Kerrigan, "he's an ideas man". I text Mick asking is it ok if the 4 of us can wait at his house, until we hear from Prof. Lind about the decompression craniectomy outcome. The rain has stopped and, as we walk across the road to watch a magnificent sunset unfold, Tracey rings and says "of course bring the kids". On such a rainy day we are surprised when a hole in the clouds miraculously appears and the sun comes out at exactly 5.20pm. Hannah takes a photo to show Glen. The kids are very comfortable talking with Tracey and Mick about Glen's condition. They know all about Tracey's own cancer struggle.

Mick is one of the smartest guys I know, plus he is an amazing listener. He always knows the right things to say at the right time. I'm assured and comforted with the incredibly diversified team of support we have, I can feel all our friends and relatives, and everyone in Bunbury wanting Glen to pull through. The boys have a beer and Hannah a glass of red wine. I can't help myself and persuade Mick to invite Hannah into the wine cellar. I'm so proud of what Mick has achieved, and his wine cellar is a testament to his success. Hannah is suitably impressed. We sit around talking, then simultaneously all freak out when the unknown number calls. It's 6.21pm. The 4 of us rush into the next room and its Professor Lind. I put him on speaker. The operation is a success! I'm crying, but trying to hold it together while the 3 kids sob with relief. Genius Lind answers all our questions. I can't believe this roller coaster is happening and Glen will never believe it. We all agree this must break the record for surgery time, before Jake Googles a team of Chinese surgeons all lying prostrate on the floor after a 36-hour single surgery. I take the kids back to the hospital where we all see Glen briefly. She looks peaceful. The swelling appears to have subsided somewhat already and ICP is 3. We separate, I drive back to Mick's house in Peppy Grove and the kids make their way to Hannah's house in Embleton.

By 10.46pm I'm falling asleep but I manage my usual meditation. After my early clumsy attempts at meditating years ago, I now lose myself easily. I don't know how others meditate, but I have been practicing my own little self-developed technique for decades now. Somehow, I fall into a place where I feel in balance and harmony easily. It works for me. I feel like the arms of God are around me and I am in total harmony with my Universe. I don't have to block anything out because there is nothing coming in. It's a time where I feel I am simply exchanging ... receiving and giving out energy. I am simply a vessel, an intermediary or facilitator if you like, for the workings and intentions of a far greater power. I begin by relaxing. Closing my eyes, I centre myself, and make my being available to my Creator. I don't think of plans. I give myself over, give my ego away. I ask the Universal Energy to inhabit me, take me over. Somehow, I arrive at a place or space where time and consciousness are irrelevant, they cease to exist. This process takes however long as it needs, then, in an instant I'm back from wherever I was, feeling a need to give thanks. I've gotten into the habit of finishing with my Lord's Prayer followed by my personal mantra. I would encourage everyone to develop their own mantra, but for what it's worth, here's mine:

"I am whole, I am complete. I am strong, I am powerful. I am loving, I am harmonious. I am open to all opportunities as they arise. I am fully receptive to all the creative energy forces in the universe as they gravitate towards me, and as I gravitate towards them. I am in control of my thoughts, I feel good and I am happy. I am fully deserving of all the incredible gifts that have been bestowed upon me throughout my life. I am also fully deserving of the fantastic gifts, amazing abundance and immense wealth that will be given me in the future. I know this is only true because I will be given the courage to accept, and the strength to receive all these gifts and use them in a charitable, considerate, kind, compassionate, generous and wise manner. I am a child of God. I am in his hands. As for my body? it was never meant to be permanent. As for my Spirit? it is immortal. Why then should I be afraid of anything."

When it's over, I offer a thank you to my God for another day with Glen, and today I hold Stewie in my heart as he sits alone at home.

I thank my God for our wonderful children. I ask for more time, for Glen, to allow her to complete fully, her reason for living. She is a light. Her unborn grandchildren want to meet her because they don't know much they need her love. I am. That's a very powerful sentence. I am, a minute part of this intricate universe, but this makes me no less important or more important than any other part. I am a part of all the parts of the universe. I feel it.

I set my alarm for 6.16am as I know Glen is fully sedated, but I wake at 6.05am. A quick shower and shave should do it. I chuckle to myself because I hear Glen saying "You don't know how to have a quick shower!" She's right of course. Whenever we're late it's because I took too long in the shower. I don't care. Sorry, but a hot shower is one of the greatest of all pleasures in a civilised society, and one I insist gets the full respect it deserves. By the time I've showered, shaved and made the bed it's 7.00am. That's not bad considering I tapped out a few words. My body is ready for the day ahead, I'm in presentable condition for whatever the Universe throws at me. I stop at la Galette de France in Hampden Road, for a quick takeaway coffee because the only decent coffee maker at SCGH won't be open this early on a Saturday, then I realise it's actually Sunday. I hope the doctors never have to ask me the concussion question ... "what day is it"? I never know. I don't feel it's necessary to know really, so long as I am aware of whatever it is I want to do that day, then that's all that matters to me.

As I approach ICU, I receive a text from Spider, another good mate I met in Africa in '74.

I respond: "Yes Spider, thanks mate. I have just arrived at ICU and was answering your text when a guy leaving stops me and introduces himself as Paul".

He says "you're Steve, aren't you? I was looking after your wife last night. She has had a good night, no pressure, stable, sleeping under sedation".
He talks with me for about 5 minutes.
He says "they intend to keep her sedated all day today and tomorrow, she should recover and we look forward to 2 good days". The level of care here is just awesome.

I am buoyed as I finally sit next to Glen at 7.40am. The nurses have combed her hair and it sits beautifully spread on the pillow. She looks peaceful, resting slightly on her left side. After changeover the new nurse is named Emma. She tells me the same story Paul just related. The coffee tastes good. Emma is busy, I like that. I notice a second nurse studying her data charts, I like that too, the more people looking after my beautiful wife the better. I've realised why I am being so specific with these diary entries. It's because I know Glen will wake up. She will find it hard to believe she has lost so much time. The world has moved on and she has been stuck in another dimension. After the initial stent was put in on March 26th, she lost a few days under anaesthetic, when she awakened she wanted to know what had happened to her, to us, and everything else. I guess it's like a Hollywood time machine movie, only this time it's a nightmare. I want her to be able to read about her remarkable lost time, and to walk in our steps throughout her journey. I want her to know of the outpouring of love from all her family, friends and total strangers praying for her. I want her to understand that we all love her, even if she comes out of this compromised in some way. I'm hoping this diary can, in some way, give her back her life. I want her to learn that when Hannah was sobbing while driving home after bad news in ICU one day, little 2.5-year-old granddaughter Marley says "why are you crying Mummy?" Hannah says "I'm crying because Grandma is a bit sick in hospital" and Marley says "don't cry Mummy, Grandma will be alright".

The more I see Emma working the more I like her. She asks me to step out while she gives Glen a back rub and she'll call me back in after. Sure enough, she calls within a short time. I go back in. She's starting to morph into Brooke. I notice she is a registered nurse just like Brooke (and indeed Hannah), not a clinical nurse. She doesn't stop working, softly talking to Glen as she works, apologising for any discomfort as she performs the response tests. We chat a bit. She's from Dunedin in NZ, managed to get a quick trip home when the Covid travel bubble was established between Australia and NZ. She repositions Glen's right arm, raises it a little, wanting the fluid build-up to minimise or reduce. It's been gloves on, gloves off a couple of times since I got here plus regular hand sanitiser. Glen's ICP is 9-10. BP is 127/60. I hate to think what her ICP would be if she hadn't had the op yesterday.

As I look at Glen I reminisce on our relationship. Glen knows dates better than me but I reckon I first met Glen in 1971. I was studying for a Diploma in Accounting and she was a student at Saint Joseph's secondary college. We were both studying in Bunbury, Western Australia. We had a group of common friends and I met Glen thru Geoff Mountford, who was studying accounting with me. Glen was a good friend of Geoff's girlfriend Cath. Glen always said I was her first love and that she always knew we would be together. I'm not going to lie. It wasn't like that for me and I broke Glen's heart a few times, many times. In my late teens, I partied hard, and wasn't committed to a long-term relationship with anyone. Glen has an un-favourite story she tells of when we went to a party together and I left with another girl. She knew I was a naughty boy and later in life we talked about it often.

We had both moved to Perth, Glen to study nursing and me to work for a group of chartered accountants on St George's Terrace. We lived quite separate lives, she lived in the nurse's quarters at Princess Margaret Hospital while I rented various share houses with other testosterone filled young men. We all lived for a good time. My personal motto became "punish your body into submission", and I did, many times. These were the days of Fatty Lumpkin, Sid Rumpo, The Dugites, army great coats and Sunday sessions at the Windsor Hotel. One of our rental homes was featured on the front page of a Perth newspaper because we nailed the letter box to the apex of the roof with the words "Air Mail" painted on it. These were pre-internet days, no mobile phones, no Facebook, no Instagram etc. When we wanted to throw a party, we would fill out a foolscap page with invitations (party, address, date, time), photocopy it a few times, then cut them up, head to the pubs and hand them out to all the prettiest girls we could find. One party in Labouchere Road in South Perth attracted about 300 people. "Sebastian", a 4-piece band living next door rehearsed Ventura Highway while Santana, Led Zeppelin, The Doors, Janis Joplin and Joe Cocker meant we were never without music, usually played thru the biggest speaker systems we could afford. When the party died, we just kept partying with lighter music - cue Neil Young, James Taylor, Carol King. I practiced singing my housemate Eddie to sleep, with Neil Diamond, Leonard Cohen and Elton John and, it was around this time I finally found the confidence to sing in front of a full audience. Anglican Dean Hazlewood, famous for The Rock Mass for Love in 1971, had opened a drop-in centre in the bowels of St Georges Cathedral. Two large brown wooden doors off St Georges Terrace opened into a basement type room with coffee, some board games, a few bean bags and rows of chairs. The guy before me did a brilliant solo version of Stairway to Heaven, the full 8 minutes. I would have left in embarrassment but he was so good I had to see the whole act. My name was called and I immediately felt woefully inadequate shuffling toward the stage. I'll never forget strumming the opening bars of So Long Marianne. The original version by Leonard Cohen has a short solo acoustic guitar intro, it's a simple pattern, quite recognizable. I'm not sure if I nailed it or whether it was a serendipitous song choice, but the crowd started clapping the moment I opened my mouth. It was a popular song, my favourite at the time and, to my surprise, quite possibly the perfect juxtaposition to Stairway to Heaven.

My friendship with Glen throughout this time was very one sided, Glen was the giver and I was the taker. In retrospect, I'm not proud of my behaviour. We were two kids growing up writing our own rule book, but it is what it is and, in the end, everything turned out exactly as Glen had seemed to instinctively know it would.

Stephen Trigwell

Leap of Faith

Before long, I realised I didn't like working in accounting. I saw a cheap airfare being advertised, $444 one way from Perth to London with an optional 12-month stopover in Johannesburg, South Africa. I booked the airfare before realising I didn't have any money to live on. Every week, I was spending every cent of my $25 pay packet on partying, vinyl albums and the best clothes I could afford. Early one morning, coming back from a party in Scarborough I ran my mate's car off the road - hit a tree. As I say, I'm not proud of a lot of things I did. Luckily, in our share house all the boys had been in accidents before, so we had a stack of insurance claim papers on hand. I decided to quit my accounting job and head down south to my parents' home in Donnybrook, to pick some fruit and make some money.

The ICU Dr Luke does his rounds. He tells me what I already know about Glen's condition but I question him on the "infarction" damage to the right side of Glen's brain. He tells me she will most likely have no movement on left side - no arm function and no leg function. This is a little more confronting than "left arm deficit and possible left leg deficit". I quiz him on potential rehab improvement and he says "well yes maybe blah blah blah" ... I decide to wait on Prof Lind's assessment. Glen is motionless. It's ok ... for now, that's what she is supposed to do.

So, I'm picking apples ... making more money than I ever did as a trainee accountant. I pay off the $300 insurance excess on Johnnies 1964 EH Holden sedan, the one I crashed into the box tree outside the army barracks on Canning Highway. I remember ringing the tow truck company from a red phone box, we had their number at the share house, then sweating on their arrival before any cops came along. Sure enough, tow truck arrives early and tows me 2 streets to the share house and the smash never happened. That was how it was in 1974.

I managed to pay the $444 airfare and flew out on 6th June 1974. This date would forever, be a special day in my life. Almost immediately, I began writing blank verse during the flight as a way of expressing how I felt, a writing habit which I grew into very comfortably. Over time, my scrap book became 2 scrap books and I began to dabble with song lyrics. I thought each jotting was deeply profound with new insight. The reality was, from a writing perspective they were bloody awful, but it's interesting for me to read them now, they paint a picture of a confused boy searching for identity, purpose and love. I realise what a lost soul I was at aged 20. Everyone grows up differently, I just did mine on paper.

I arrived in Joburg with A$1000, equivalent to $1000 Rand. My partying went up a few levels and as I'm strutting down Kotze Street, my feet are not touching the ground. I'm floating like never before. I stayed the first week in St Tropez apartments - sounds exotic but in reality, a multi storied brick block of flats. I was sharing with Carol Mitchison and Terri Bennison, two girls from Sydney, and another guy Kevin Cornish, also from Sydney. Two single beds, four people, quite an interesting week. Two weeks in and six of us piled into a hired Kombi and drove to Kruger National Park. We spend the first night in a rondaaval in Shingwidzi, one of the park camps.

I'm hearing all sorts of weird animal noises, so I ask a ranger "why is the fence so low?" ... "to keep the tourists in" he replies. I sampled the lunch menu for my scrapbook: Shingwidzi 20.6.74. Good Afternoon. Lunch R1.20. Choice of baked fish with fine herbs or, grilled rump steak with mashed potatoes and vegetables or, cold meat and salads. Followed by lemon snow and custard, cheese and biscuits, tea or coffee. Not bad for R1.20. Don't ask me what lemon snow is. I met so many people in those first few weeks, some would become lifelong friends, every day filled with new smells, new food, new music, new places, faces, pubs, clubs, new parties.

My mate Simmy decides he too wants out of Australia, and leaving Perth on August 31st, he flies into the coldest Joburg spring in 50 years. I'd known Simmy since primary school in the small country town of Brunswick Junction in South Western Australia. His father managed the biggest business in town - Peters Creameries, and my Dad was the Officer in Charge at Brunswick Police Station. Together with the bank manager's son Johnny Luscombe (I smashed his car), we made a formidable three amigos living a huckleberry finn type existence on the banks of the Brunswick River. We shared our first clandestine cigarettes together, our first illegal drive in a car, and our first clumsy attempts at trying to impress the same girls at the same parties. During summer holidays we learnt to swim in the river and picked wild blackberries from our homemade corrugated iron canoes. Every Friday night we'd race our slot cars around a massive 8 lane track, competing amongst virtually every kid in town. Life was good in sleepy Brunswick.

On Simmy's first night in Joburg, we inadvertently find ourselves listening to a great live band performing Elton John's Rocket Man and Don't Let the Sun Go Down on Me. It takes us all night to realise we are two guys sitting in the Butterfly Bar of the Skyline

Hotel. History records the Butterfly in 1974 as the go to place for gays and lesbians. We enjoyed the fantastic band and the Lion Lager, no-one hit on us ... maybe they thought we were partners? We rented together at 606 DoRomo apartments in Hillbrow. From my recollections, the Hillbrow, Berea area was the most populated square kilometre in the Southern Hemisphere at the time. I can believe it. The Chelsea Pub and The Ambassador spring to mind as other venues we regularly visited. We've now got 2 guitars ... and a marijuana plant growing in our wardrobe. Every day I take the plant and place it in the sunshine near the window. In between teaching Simmy how to play guitar, we sunbake beside the rooftop pool, playing monopoly, and taking turns timing our leaps to water bomb cars at the traffic lights below.

Simmy gets a job working for British Industrial Calendar Cables - BICC, and I sign with temporary agency Manpower. My first job is working for Johannesburg Hat Mills. I can't remember my role there, can't remember making any hats, can't remember doing any real work there to be honest. I place a small classified ad in the Johannesburg Star, "Young Aussie backpacker looking for a job, will do anything, likes big dogs and kids". I hate to think of the weirdos I'd get if I posted an ad like that these days. I received one reply and attended an interview in the 50-storey high Carlton Centre downtown. South Africa was only just preparing for the introduction of television in 1974, and the interviewer asks "we are looking for stunt men, can you ride a horse?" "Can I ride a horse? Of course, I can - I come from a farm don't I!". "Good" he says, "we're going to send you to stunt school, where after 3 weeks, you'll fall off a 3-story building ... backwards". Ah, no thanks. Maybe I should've said yes! Who knows where that sliding door would have taken me. To this day I've never ridden a horse in my life. The closest I've been is watching vertically challenged people in fancy dress whip the shit out of them as they run around in a circle. Strange sport.

On the corner opposite the Chelsea Pub there was another live music bar called the Park Lane. One night the solo guitarist is playing something I obviously wasn't enjoying and I'm getting frustrated. I can't take him meandering through the motions any more so, I leap up and say "Give me that guitar man". I'm on stage and fired up to slay the crowd, then realise I'm a fucking ballad man! I'm the guy who plays Neil Young at the end of the night. All I had was Elton John's Crocodile Rock, and it's a 12-string guitar, which I'd never played before. I go for it anyway and the crowd goes off, yelling "yeah! more! more" ... and I realise I haven't got any more! So, I learnt a couple of valuable lessons that night - impetuosity will often get you everywhere and, in the entertainment business, always leave them hanging. I met Danny and Tom Hunt at The Park Lane that night. More on Tom later.

I suddenly get a feeling of guilt. Why am I reminiscing like this when my wife lies motionless beside me? Why am I remembering all these things that I did without her? I look out the window. It's a grey day, nimbus clouds everywhere but a beautiful rainbow shines over Nedlands and the hospital is bathed in sunlight. I am convinced we can do this. Russell calls me ... he knows this trench too. His beloved Dockers got up last night to win by 2 points, I'm happy for him. He asks about Glen and the kids. I realise that I am a member of a family that is made special because of the people that went before us, my Mum and Dad and extended family members. We were all blessed to be raised in a constant loving environment, a mixture of discipline, fun, education and instruction, inspiration, adventure and encouragement. If we stepped out of line we expected to be in big trouble, from either our own parents or the parents of our best friends. Joint parenting if you will. I go back and gently caress Glen's hand, tell her I love her one more time, and I realise she is, even now still teaching me about love.

Simmy and I hitchhike through the Eastern Transvaal, for no real reason other than to take a look. We get picked up by a guy driving a Jag. He owns a metal engineering works in Joburg and offers us a job when we're back in town. He's doing 240 kilometres an hour while chatting to us ... I'm shitting myself, it's the fastest I've ever been in my life. We play a few songs for the street kids in Machadadorp, before eventually pitching our tent on the banks of the Sabie River and exploring Pilgrims Rest ... well the Pilgrims Rest Hotel anyway. On the way back to Joburg we wake to find we've pitched our tent on the front lawn of an office block in Ermelo. It's late October back in Joburg and I spend $90 of my last few Rand on a black leather jacket. We're talking ultra-soft goat leather, satin lined, long sleeved, studs, no epaulettes, no cuffs. That's equivalent to 75 lunches at Shingwidzi ... 75 lemon snows! It was worth it. This jacket becomes my Magic Jacket.

Tommy Hunt, from my debut cameo concert at the Park Lane, was an electrician from Dorsett, England and was working on the new Afrikaans University in Braamfontein. He organised me an interview with Siemens for a high paid job as an electrician. Of course, I knew nothing about electricity, except that it could kill you. Tom said "just tell them your papers are being sent across from Australia and that you've been working on 3 phase and conduit". Tom reckoned "they'll just stick you in the ceiling cavity and you'll never have to do anything". I repeated his words of wisdom and got the job. Luckily, I left Joburg before taking it up, thereby saving a few students from certain electrocution I'm sure.

I did fall in love in Joburg, or at least what I thought was love. I had taken a temporary agency job as accountant for Nashua and was reconciling accounts for clients who had leased copying machines. The books were a disaster but I dived right in. As the doors to the elevator opened, there she was at the desk, and that was it, lust at first sight. Unfortunately, Marilyn was married and our relationship consisted of secret lunches, secret movies, secret rendezvous, secret everything really. One time her black belt karate expert husband planned a business trip to Cape Town, so I took the bus to the suburbs and stayed the night at her place. He unexpectedly rang early the next day on his way home, minutes away from the house, so I literally dived out the bedroom window as he returned. I told you I was shallow, did I mention weak willed and self-centred? That relationship was a tad explosive and eventually petered out when I headed south. Decades later it would inspire me to write a song called "Don't You Turn Around". As an aside, my mate Simmy eventually married Marilyn. It was a brief marriage and probably a mistake on both sides, as they busted up soon after. It was his second marriage after he and Frances divorced. Fran was an air hostess with SAA, a vibrant, fiery redhead with an infectious and totally fun personality. She always played her signature song on guitar, Catch the Wind, by Donovan. On 10th November 1974, Simmy threw me a surprise 21st birthday party at Fran's apartment in Berea. As we approached Fran's door, I couldn't work out why there were so many young people partying on the balcony. It was a massive, fun night. Fran knew a lot of people in the gay community and we were introduced to Cedric and Tammy. As a couple, they were two very wonderful, fun loving guys. One night we all dressed up ... and I mean dressed up, made up, hair teased out (I had the full Barry Gibb hair then), and we headed out to Shapirellis nightclub. Cedric wore a classy white hat with a wide brim. He was easy to spot because he was tall, even easier to spot when he was on the table dancing. Cedric knew we were both straight, and literally protected our arses that night.

I'd met a guy called Peter Hemphill from Queensland. One day, Danny, Tom and I piled into his Monaro and we drove east to Swaziland. We had no real destination in mind, just basically east then south. By the time we reached the border it was dark and very late. The Swazi casino was the only place open but they refused us entry. Can't blame them really. We find what looks like a nightclub with some lights flashing. As we enter the music is loud, the place is packed with young people and we think this will be fun! Within minutes we are approached by some white women who explain it is a church organised "disco" and we are most definitely not welcome. Again, can't blame them really. Eventually, we stumble upon a wedding reception and they celebrate our arrival like we are long lost friends. After some frenetic dancing with total strangers we all camp in the bushes somewhere. We continued south through Zululand, had a crazy time in Durban climbing through a window to crash a New Year's Eve function at the Fairhaven Hotel, discovered the Durban Markets and DP (Durban Poison marijuana), as well as somehow, finding a suburban party with the obligatory live band before leaving Natal.

As young Aussie backpackers, we were all politically naïve and totally oblivious to the political turmoil in South Africa at the time. Later in life, after reading Nelson Mandela's Long Road to Freedom, I realised we had travelled at a very repressive time. The Rivonia Trials were completed in 1963-64 of course, and Nelson Mandela, along with most of the other ANC leaders in the fight against racism and apartheid, were in jail. There was a relative lull in social unrest prior to Steve Biko's assassination in 1977. During 1974, the South African Police, or SAP was in iron clad control, every backpacker knew not to get in their way. We were all totally unaware that through circumstance and timing, it was a relatively innocuous time for a bunch of backpacking white larrikins to be footloose and fancy free in South Africa.

The bitumen quickly faded to dirt road upon entering the Transkei, one of ten Black Homelands designated by the white dominated government in Pretoria. Later in life, I would read the Homelands were given sham independence, which served as a means of forced removal and denial of political rights to black South Africans. As we turned off the main road to Umtata, we stopped at a small roadside pub along the winding road to Port St John's on the coast. As soon as we entered the bar, we knew we were not welcome when the few barflies seated turned, and stared in our direction. We didn't understand that whites were not welcome in the Homeland. The bartender was kind enough to sell us a carton and we left. I reckon we arrived in Port St John's just before they started filming Shout at The Devil with Lee Marvin and Roger Moore, as the sets were on site. Damn, I could have been a stunt man for Roger Moore! … fuck, I could have even *been* Roger Moore! We camped under the shade of huge fig trees where monkeys were plentiful and adept at stealing food and anything else that wasn't nailed down. We stayed there about a week, before leaving the Wild Coast, for two days in East London then on to Port Elizabeth.

My time in Port Elizabeth, or PE as we all called it, would be pivotal in my life. It's the first place I ran out of money and where Spider took pity, leaving his half-eaten honey sandwiches for me to eat. It's where I auditioned for my first ever pub gig. I never got the gig, so Homer retaliated by smashing a bottle on the bar and ordered a stack of beers on the house. It's where we filmed a classic super 8 video on the sands of Van Stadens beach and, where we partied at

Una's house with everyone phoning home while Cyril, the shearer from Northam, distracted Una lying naked in her bath. It's where Kenny Reynolds would open and eat a can of pet food while casually working the room having conversations with total strangers. It's where one night we discovered Limbo cane spirit at the Fuckowie cricket and rugby club and literally all got lost. I learnt to hustle to survive in PE and by co-incidence, where I actually saved a man's life. It's where I would meet amazing people who would become lifelong friends.

Havelock Square was an enclave of residential houses surrounding a square section of road, at the top of the grassy knoll which was Donkin Hill. Looking east, the hill offered a commanding view of the city, past the neat row of colonial whitewashed terraced houses tumbling downhill on the left, over the 40-metre-high Campanile Tower near the wharf and out across the bay. 1a Havelock Square never felt owned by anybody really ... we paid rent, but the constant stream of backpackers coming and going, some for one night, some for a week, meant 1a took on a life of its own. We had a lovely housekeeper by the name of Esme. She was short and stocky, usually dressed in blue, and every day, she began her day by cleaning up the marijuana evidence from the night before, usually two or three ashtrays, a few stray leaves and maybe some Union Jack papers. By this stage most of the boys were shift working at the Port, either as forklift drivers, crane drivers or tally clerks. Esme never had to pick her way around sleeping bodies on the floor as the early shift started pre-dawn, and those taking the twenty-minute walk down the hill needed to be away in the pitch black, well before sunrise. My application for a work visa to work on the wharf took longer than all the others. I was absolutely flat broke. I even sold the Magic Jacket. Spider bought it off me, he loved it. So, again, Spider saved my monetary arse. I knew the jacket was going to a good home. Down at the wharf I watched closely, as the other visas came through and were granted. I took note that upon request for visa information, A.G. Nel would leave his desk and walk into a back room to check for telex messages. A.G. Nel was a huge, slow moving hulk, with the weariness of thirty years in an ignominious desk job. If the visa had been approved he would return, open his top left drawer, retrieve a stamp and proceed to stamp, then sign the imprint in the relevant passport. I watched this process every day for 2 weeks. Nervously, one day when he went to the back room I opened the drawer, stamped my own passport and high tailed it out of there before he returned. I could forge his signature easily as everyone else had the same visa, same signature. I got a job as a tally clerk, recording pallet loads of goods as they were craned off the ships. We were supposed to report the black guys if we saw them stealing stuff but we never bothered. The giveaway was a steady stream of workers, surreptitiously making their way to the same remote section of the warehouse. Once, I weakened and somehow, some Brut deodorant and a fancy lace tablecloth found their way under the false bottom of my airways carry bag. Every backpacker needs a fancy lace tablecloth. I sent it back to my Mum in Australia.

One time I was working night shift, it's about three o'clock in the morning and we are unloading cartons of Johnnie Walker whisky. Suddenly, there is a huge commotion and about thirty guys are crowded on the wharf pointing and yelling in Xhosa. I look into the deep, black water, out past the massive bulbous bow of the ship sitting above water level, and they are yelling "boss, boss ... it's a wop", at least that's what I thought they were saying. I thought it was a seal but, in the gloom, I could see a man floating face down, arms outstretched and not moving. I quickly stripped to my jocks and dived in. As soon as I hit the water I panicked a little ... can I do this? I swam to where the spotlight was shining on his motionless body. I thought for sure I was retrieving a dead guy. I'm remembering my childhood Bronze Medallion lessons in the freezing Brunswick river and, as I get to him, flip him over and start the reasonably long and arduous swim back I'm holding him up with my right arm and hip. Slowly, I'm side stroking my way back to the wharf when suddenly, he violently vomits and starts flaying his arms around. I'm starting to really struggle now, but just manage to push him into a net they had craned over the side of the wharf. They lift him up and throw me down a rope ... but not any rope, we're talking a fucking rope you tie ships up with, it's massive, with barnacles and no fucking knots for leverage. Where's *my* fucking net! I'm exhausted and can't climb, so I just hang on like shark bait until they lower me the net. By the time I'm lifted he's gone, and so are all my clothes, stolen. My favourite black cheesecloth embroidered hippie top I bought downstairs in Trinity Arcade, Perth, gone. The harbour was deep, but I was still shallow. The big boss Mr. Van de Merwe (I kid you not) interviews me ... "I wouldn't have saved him" he says. "He was totally pissed on Johnnie Walker, bugger him". I can't remember what I wore home.

After that, I became a bit of a hero with the Xhosas and I remember a marvellous man, Livingstone, trying to teach me how to speak the language. A very gentle man, Livingstone knew planes. Every plane flying over PE, the airline, flight path, the destination, take-off and landing times, Livingstone knew them all. We would sit and watch the sun rising orange, red and yellow, flickering on the ocean as it turned from black to blue and green. By now, most of my Aussie party mates from 1a Havelock Square had flown to England and I'm banking as fast as I can to join them. Africa from 6th June 1974 became 364 days of my life. My 12-month visa expired the day after

I flew to London. Simmy stayed of course, and with Fran had a son Stephen. Yes, I'm proud to say he was named after me and today, is a well-known successful writer living and working in Cape Town. Simmy stayed in Africa for 42 years before he would return home. Home, to Australia.

The kids all know the plan for Glen today, they are resting while I sit here and tap away with one finger, while my other hand rests on Glen's cold right foot. The woman in the ICU bed next to us is waking up from sedation, trying to pull the ventilator out. She's aggressive. It sounds bad, the nurses are firm but caring. I steel myself a bit because one day this may be Glen. I'm feeling some trepidation for what lies ahead ... coming out of sedation, response or lack thereof, how will Glen be? will she know me? are my expectations valid? I quickly stop myself and realise I can only control my thoughts, nothing else, so it is my thoughts that are causing this trepidation. I change my thoughts and immediately I sense Glen's cold foot is now warm. It's 11.35am and I get a tap on my shoulder, it's Dylan. We exchange news and he quizzes the nurse on Glen's condition. He's very specific and his medical vocabulary has expanded, he sounds like a neuro surgeon. Dyl suggests I take a couple of hours off, relax and watch the Eagles play GWS while he sits with his Mum. I take the opportunity because I know Glen is in good hands. Before I get to the first roundabout I'm thinking "why am I doing this? why am I writing all this down? why has it morphed from simply recording tablets, headaches and sleep patterns into something so much more? why am I putting my life story into this?" As I burst into tears again, I realise that except for my childhood, my whole life has been Glen. Every step, every birth, every death, every car, every house, every holiday, every work day. We've shared every memory. So, when she wakes up, she needs to know every thought I've had while she's been asleep, so she can catch up on all this lost time. She can rebuild her memory. We will all rebuild her memory, one laugh at a time, one tear at a time. Hopefully of course, she won't have lost any memory other than this hospital time. So, as I'm driving, I'm crying, because I realise Glen is going to ask "what did you do every day, what's happened?" and I'm going to say "well I wrote a book! You've been under for so long I actually wrote a WHOLE FUCKING BOOK!" She's not going to believe it and nor do I.

Money, it's a Gas

I flew into Heathrow, but didn't stay in London before hitchhiking to Poole, in Dorsett on the South coast, with Kenny Reynolds, another Perth Aussie who took the $444 cheap airfare thru Africa. I'm wearing my new denim patch jacket and it's me, backpack and guitar, with Ken, versus the traffic on the M3. No one stops. Suddenly, Ken starts doing handstands on the roadside and a car stops immediately. All the amazing people I met when backpacking the world had a fantastic spirit of abandon and adventure. Later in life, many of the guys went on to become very successful businessmen. All of us have remained firm friends. Mick was my best man when I married, Spider was a groomsman. Party time lifted another level again in Poole. Spider fell in love with my denim patch jacket so I jumped at the opportunity to do a swap. The Magic Jacket was back with its rightful owner.

I did a lot of busking in Poole. Mick and I positioned ourselves where the walkway bridge crossed the suburban rail line. As crowds built up I would run through about 4-5 songs, usually Daniel by Elton John, Sorrow or Five Years by David Bowie, Ladbroke Grove by Leo Sayer, maybe American Pie. I had a solo repertoire of about 100 songs. Mick would dress in his scruffiest clothes and, with chewed paper cup in hand, put the hard word on passers-by. I must say, to this day I always give support and a few bucks to serious buskers, although I'm sure having the specialist beggar out front makes all the difference. One time, a father sitting at the Wimpy Bar opposite sent his young daughter across with a nice compliment and a pound note to stuff into the paper cup. Mick never worked with a cup full of money, always taking cash out as we didn't want to appear to be going too well. After we made a few pounds we'd go down to the waterfront, The Sail and Anchor or The Jolly Sailor to drink up the profits.

The Eagles lose to GWS 93 to 77 and I tell myself it's not a big deal in the scheme of life. At 2.04pm Hannah calls and says she has taken over from Dylan at Glen's bedside and for me not to rush back. At 3.36pm I get her text: "All good here, Mum sleeping peacefully. BP120/60, ICP 8". I pull into the hospital car park at 3.56pm and it occurs to me Dylan's theory of Google Maps and the human mind might have some legs to it. Since Glen has been in hospital I've had to re-learn many of the Perth road networks ... and I'm finally getting it. Glen may have to re learn many things, not sure, but I know we can have fun doing it. You never know, she might be one of those stories you hear about on social media; "Woman in coma for 2 weeks, wakes up speaking fluent Spanish, reading concert music and nagging husband over driving". I've noticed how, over the last few days we've all used humour to break the tension that builds after a major op. Bad news leads into the heartbreak of having to decide a course of action, the incredible stress while the op is actually underway, and then the nightmare unknown phone number call, waiting for a result. The cue for all of us to burst into tears and hug each other is always the unknown number. I am definitely changing my call signal when this is all over. Every time it goes off we all freak out. It has seriously taken on a new meaning. It's 6.19pm, Dylan has come and gone again. He took the opportunity to visit his mate Rob who lives nearby.

I once wrote a song called The Masterplan. I liked it. Glen hated it. Friends hated it. Everybody hated it. It's a song about ransoms and the trade-offs we make in our lives in a sacrificial attempt to get some reward. At the time, one of our children was desperately trying for a child. After huge difficulties there was a pregnancy then, tragically, they lost the baby. They were devastated and Glen and I felt helpless. Later that night I began the "trade off conversation" with my God ... you know "Please God help me out and I'll sacrifice this". By the time one reaches trade off stage, the sacrifice is inevitably substantial. Interestingly, nowadays I don't do trade-offs. I am content with what my God deals me. I figure if I'm a good person, then my karma will be commensurate and God will look after me. Since Glen has been in hospital though, one of my sons confided in me his trade off conversation. "I made a deal with God" he says. "I told him if Mum pulls through this, bitcoin can go to zero". It's a big ransom and, as I write, Bitcoin has already gone down hard from $US 60k to ~$US 30k. I knew that deep down, money and Bitcoin really meant nothing to this young man, even though he thought he believed they did. Even before Glen's condition manifested itself, I knew when compared to real values like the love and health of his family, material things didn't count to him. He knew it too, he just didn't realise he knew it too. His karma is good anyway. He has no worries, and Bitcoin will one day go to the moon, I just don't know when. Buy it. (usual disclaimer- not financial advice, dyor, never gamble more than you can afford to lose, don't smoke and don't wear lycra).

Glen's ICP 11. BP 125/57. All good in la-la land. Mick texts me and asks if I'm going to duck back there for dinner. I text

Hannah an update on Glen and they all decide it's a good idea. I arrange to call ICU for an update just before I nod off tonight, and for them to call me immediately if there are any problems. I don't tell the kids it's wagyu steak, not any old wagyu either, Boatshed wagyu cooked by Mick is the best steak I have ever tasted in my life. I realise I'm starting to sound like Glen! I'm suddenly awake at 1.10am with a frightening sense of apprehension. I tell myself Steve you're being silly, but decide to call ICU anyway, waiting to get put through I have an anxious foreboding, I'm instantly calmed when her nurse Debbie tells me she is fine, no change. I answer a text from my mate Pete in Vancouver. In my mind I have gathered together an army of impressive magnitude to carry Glen, and us through this valley. I'm reminded of my Mother's battle in her darkest hours and I'm instantly calmed, because I know my Mum will lift Glen up. They are all helping. My parents, her parents, all the rellies before, all our friends, various prayer groups, people on the other side of the world. We are unstoppable. A quick wee for the 67-year-old bloke and it's back to sleep.

Alarm goes off at 6.15am. Thank you God. I have a quick shower (that's a joke for you Glen), and I realise I've forgotten to bring my towel into the bathroom. No problem "Glen! Can you bring me another towel please?" It's raining hard as I drive from McNeill Street Peppermint Grove, down Stirling Highway to the hospital. I'm pondering Dylan's Google Maps theory again. What if we extend that same concept to quantum entanglement? What if the human brain is quantum entangled with everything outside the brain? Not just maps, I mean everything in the Universe. In other words, we know and are connected to everything. We've just forgotten the connection. I'm pretty sure this is exactly what Dylan meant, it just takes me time to process. His theory sits well with STEM. More on STEM later. I decide immediately it's undoubtedly true, fits in with common sense, atomic and quantum physics, explains $E=MC^2$ and is compatible with all religious dogmas. Simple. Piece of piss.

In between the raindrops, I imagine a whole new reality TV show. It's called ICU Nurse. We have hidden cameras in ICU and nurses are assessed by a remote team of virtual judges and AI data recorders. The constant turnover of nurses means a never-ending supply of contestants. So far Brooke is winning hands down. By the time I pull up in the car park I'm chiding myself for driving past la Galette de France and not grabbing a coffee. Another few hours of stability are confirmed by ICU nurse Debbie when I am allowed in at 7.05am. Glen looks peaceful, ICP is 8 and BP is 129/68. Changeover occurs and the new contestant is ... Lauren! Not long after, they ask me to step outside "we need to do a few things" that's ok, I understand they are working hard.

About 8 of us piled into a Kombi and drove across Southern England to Holyhead, in Anglesey, Wales. We'd all been staying at Tom Hunt's house in Hamworthy near Poole. Tom had been invited to a wedding in Ireland and somehow, we'd all managed an invitation. I'd been backpacking now for about a year, playing guitar and singing every day, often for parties and in odd pubs. I was comfortable in front of a crowd. The wedding reception was held in Boyle and I was wearing the Magic Jacket and flared denims. Half way thru the night, we're all smashed on free Irish beer and the band is playing the Unicorn song by the Irish Rovers. I snapped. Seriously, the Unicorn song would snap anybody. Next minute I'm on stage fronting the band with someone else's guitar and again, can't believe I did this twice, I realise I'm not a Rock n Roll performer ... fuck it, but by now

I'm seasoned enough to recover and I count the band in for Blue Suede Shoes by Elvis. They didn't even know what song I was going to play (nor did I actually), but I knew they'd be ok as it's an old standard and there are only 3 chords in it. Anyway, the crowd goes nuts and that was it. One song. It's out of my system and I'm happy. I'm back drinking free Irish beer with the boys when a middle-aged American woman comes over and says straight up "I love Elvis, saw him in Vegas, that was amazing", we chat a little then it's "can we go outside and have sex in your van"? I was 21. I was single. I was immature. Why not? In hindsight, I'm very glad her friend came over and gently talked her and me out of it. I could go on with my shallowness, but I'd probably end up on the beach.

On 5th July, 1975 Tommy Hunt, Mick and I joined 100,000 concert goers at Knebworth for a massive concert headlined by Pink Floyd, The Steve Miller Band and Captain Beefheart. It was billed as the first concert to feature a quadrophonic speaker system and Pink Floyd's opening song was Money, from Dark Side of The Moon, the album had not long been released. The cash registers at the start of the song were electrifying, and I'm sure the guy walking around selling LSD, acid and dope from his shoulder harness heard the real cachink, cachink all day long, he did a massive trade.

My stay in the UK ended abruptly in August 1975. Mick and I were taken in by Poole Police as witnesses against Tom's alleged importation of marijuana from Africa. The constabulary had their sights set on putting Tom in jail. In separate interrogations, detectives threatened both Mick and I with 10 years in Winchester prison if we didn't comply and sign their prepared statements. Under duress and shitting ourselves, we signed. We were immediately released, with our passports. Early next morning, we withdrew our statements and decided to skip the country. That night, about 1am,

Mick and I made a secret dash for Southampton. We hired a cab, an unthinkable waste of money for a couple of fine upstanding young backpackers. We were freaking out in the back seat, constantly worried we were being followed. Nervously, we made the ferry and, after a tense journey arrived in Le Havre, France, where we immediately jumped on a train to Paris. Disembarking into a crowded Gare de Nord railway station, we figured our newfound urban anonymity had successfully sealed our escape. I have no memory of Paris at all really, totally missed the Montmartre, the Eiffel Tower and the Arc de Triomphe, I don't think we stayed in the city at all, before catching another train south. Our intention was to make Spain as it was considered cheap to live there. Our trip came to an abrupt halt in Lyon, the train simply stopped. Exhausted, Mick and I rolled out our sleeping bags on the platform of the Lyon train station, crashing for the night. Changing train, the next day we managed to elude any ticket collectors by watching their movements and hiding in the toilets at the appropriate times. We travelled the entire country from Le Havre to Perpignan, without paying a fare and without getting caught, eventually reaching the small Spanish town of Llansa, north of Barcelona. We pitched our 2-man tent in a small seaside caravan camping park, before heading to the bar for a few red wines and an impromptu guitar session with a stranger sitting in the corner. I think he was German. We couldn't understand each other, but with music as the international language, I soon learnt to toggle my first 12 bar blues. Before long, the whole bar was having a great time. It's amazing how many free drinks you get when you are the entertainers. It was only later we discovered UK police had Interpol looking for us, before they eventually dropped all charges against Tom. Luckily, global Interpol headquarters were based in Lyon ... they would never look for us there.

It's 8.46am. I'm getting a bit anxious so I pick up the handset for ICU. "No sorry, everything is ok but still a few things to do". It's quite distressing sitting in the ICU waiting room - not just because I'm not by Glen's bedside, but also because one cannot avoid seeing other families going through the same horrible experience as us. Tears flow freely. I feel so sorry for them too. I'm back in at 9.00am. Glen looks calm ICP 10, BP 147/69. The new contestant Lauren goes for a break and Shelby temporarily takes over. Hannah texts, she wants to come in but I tell her Glen is booked for a scan at 10am and we won't be allowed back in until maybe 11.30am so she decides to wait until then. While this is going on an alarm starts beeping on Glen's monitor. I'm searching for Shelby, she's not around. I'm frantically looking at the monitor trying to figure out the problem and I see Glen's BP has risen to 159/94 ... I can't see Shelby anywhere then suddenly, she appears from the room opposite. She comes over and soothes my nerves with "everything is fine, it's just a balance between sedation and adrenaline". She adjusts the adrenaline down to 4mg/hr. Within minutes her BP is down to 120/57. ICP 11. I'm calm. In talking with Lauren and Riley her able assistant, it unfolds we are all from Bunbury. That makes me feel good, and I think Glen would like that. It's 9.48am and Glen is about to go for her scan - not back at 11.39am so I'll pop out and grab a coffee. In my mind I've just been through France and Spain so the menu at la Galette de France keeps me in European mode. Shall I go the Crepe Monsieur, a Nicoise Salad or maybe Duck Confit? There is a chill in the air so I settle on a bowl of French Onion soup ... coffee can wait.

Mick and I are rapidly running out of money so we decide to head to Madrid. Why? I don't know. I have a vague recollection of going to the Australian Consulate there and getting an allowance or funding of some sort. Life was pretty amazing then - the whole time I was in England the UK Govt paid me £8.16 a week for being an unemployed busking backpacker. Maybe the UK Government felt guilty about sending so many convicts down under. Enroute to Madrid we visit Figueres, birthplace of Salvatore Dali and marvelled at some of his artwork in the town museum. We shared the cheapest pensione we could find in Madrid, upstairs on a busy wide boulevard. I can't remember the street name. I started giving Mick guitar lessons and it wasn't long before he was threatening to throw the instrument out of the window. Little did he know one day he would become an accomplished gypsy guitarist and play in a workshop ensemble with the celebrated Hank Marvin. We lived on bread, cheese, mortadella and beer. I went to the bank and wired home for A$716. I knew I had the money there for my return trip. A few days went by and I was getting desperate as the money hadn't arrived. Finally, the teller gives me the money, all A$116 of it! They hadn't put the little "dash" thru the 1 to make it a 7, as is customary in some parts of Europe. I was devastated but we quickly dismissed that emotion and celebrated on the town. I bought a new pair of denim jeans with more pockets than I could count. I was pretty skinny then, probably fitted into a size 28. When I finally got the $716, I left my electric shaver with Mick, saying "Mick, if you get into real trouble I want you to pawn the shaver". Mick always chuckles when he relates the story of the shaver. We laughed about that story again last night, as we tucked into the wagyu steak. My stopover in Rome is only memorable because of all the armed militia on guard against The Red Brigades, and the fact I had no money at all to pay the airport tax. A very kind person waiting in line behind me paid my tax for me. So, I'm back in Perth and it takes a scruffy, long haired guitar carrying backpacker 2.5 hrs to hitch hike from

Perth airport to Donnybrook. I love this country. It's good to be home!

A quick ham and cheese baguette with coffee and it's back to the car park where I meet Hannah and we take the green lifts to 4th floor. It's great to see little Lennon again, he's so happy, smiling and giggling, like an island amongst the organised chaos and mayhem of ICU. Jake and Dylan arrive so it's the 4 of us when they let us in. Jake and I go first ... BP 121/57, ICP 12. Lauren tells us they are reducing the Propofol sedation ... ideally, they would want her to start waking up in 24 hrs or so. Apparently, too long on a ventilator can result in a longer than necessary hospital stay. Again, we'll wait for Prof Lind's assessment but Glen looks calm after her scan. Jake tells Glen about Tegan's text, when she takes a shower she can feel their unborn baby kicking now. I visualise Glen reading that sentence with excitement and joy. Jake and I swap with Dylan and Hannah ... and while I'm in the waiting room Rodger pops in. He seems to have really taken a special interest in Glen and our family. Before starting his shift in High Dependency Unit (HDU), he decides to see if any of us are around in the ICU waiting room. I tell him when all this chaos is over I'll try to arrange an opportunity for him to spend a couple of days at the Abrolhos on Johnnies boat. Not a done deal of course, but I don't think Johnny would mind.

Mick returned to Australia in late August 1975. I never did find out if he pawned the shaver but, we both knew we had unfinished business before we could truly unpack the backpack. The two of us would spend about 7 months in Australia before heading off again, this time to Canada. I worked continually without break, putting in long hours over the summer in my parent's takeaway food shop in Donnybrook. While living with my parents saving money, on one of my few weekends off I find time to drive to Pinjarra, for a party and champagne breakfast with Johnny Luscombe. The same weekend, the day after the party, Doug Basham's girlfriend Sharon cuts herself badly on broken glass from a smashed beer jug, as his crowded Kombi lurches drunkenly home from the Ravenswood Hotel. The irony of my 21year old bullet proof attitude is not lost on me, as I sit in the ICU waiting room surrounded by tearful relatives of accident victims.

I decide to grab 2 hrs rest while Dylan and Jake sit in ICU. A quick drive to McNeill St and I'm asleep for 1.5 hrs then back at Glen's bedside at 3.45pm. The boys have kept notes for me and I see super nurse Brooke is back on the ward, I hope she is assigned to Glen. I'm feeling really positive now. In conversation with Jake, and with a tear in her eye, nurse Riley confides she was born at St John of God hospital in Bunbury. It transpires there is a very real chance that Glen delivered her into this world. The ICU duty Doctor Brad comes around and gives the opinion on this morning's scan. Pressure has reduced as expected due to effects of the decompression craniectomy and the good (left) side of Glen's brain appears to be ok. We know there is already damage to the right brain side, however at this stage it appears no change and too early to predict severity of the loss. The plan going forward is to keep Glen sedated at ~50 mg/hr Propofol and lower it somewhat tomorrow morning and monitor her reaction to that. As it reduces they expect her to awaken. It's possible, however she may not wake for some time, and Brad says the Propofol strategy could ensue for another day (after tomorrow) but ultimately, they would want her to wake up at the end of that time. ICP 10, BP 119/54

I meet Mick in late March 1976, in Hay Street Mall, Perth. We watch the movie Jaws, before teaming up with Johnny and Doug for a road trip across the Nullarbor heading for Sydney. Mick and I planned to continue on to Canada via Hawaii. I partnered Johnny in his pretty cool Triumph sports car and Mick was with Doug in his VW kombi. Johnny's Triumph was a way better car than the EH sedan I smashed into the box tree. We made it to Kalgoorlie and partied hard for a day or 2. On about the 3rd day we go the Kalgoorlie horse races and Mick tells me he's down to his last $90. This is the spirit of adventure I spoke of earlier. Canada on $90! He puts the whole lot on a horse called Irish Pride. It's at long odds, in the last race of the day. This is the spirit of abandon I spoke of earlier. Of course, Irish Pride wins and Mick re-finances his entire trip to Canada with a bit extra. I'm not going to recount the 3934-kilometre journey from Perth to Sydney, other than to say it was one of the longest parties I've ever been on. Listening to Paul McCartney's Venus and Mars on 8 track rotation, Johnny and I would roll the seat back to change drivers without stopping the car. Why? I've got no idea. Then, under a starlit southern sky the 4 of us, together with "Scarface", a chance encounter at the front bar, partied around a campfire in Balladonia before drinking the worst beer in the world, Southwark, in South Australia. We rode the new bitumen Nullarbor road before it was open to the public, then did an early morning runner from the Hay caravan park, the owner managing to chase Doug down because his kombi was too slow.

As any young Aussie male would do, upon reaching Sydney we went straight to Bondi beach and bought chicken and chips. A seagull swooped in and stole the carcass as we lay on the sloped grass. In slow motion, Jonathon Livingstone Seagull carried the carcass high in the air before giving it up under the weight and dropping it ...

right beside two lovely young ladies sun baking alone, about 100 metres from us. They looked around bewildered, we laughed, they laughed. It was weird but then again, lots of stuff is weird. In a fitting final conclusion to our road trip across Australia, Qantas called our names as we almost missed our flight to Hawaii, sitting in the bar, drinking one last Aussie beer in the departure lounge.

Stephen Trigwell

Déjà vu

Before we knew it, there we were in Honolulu. Just like Madrid really ... not much money, nowhere to live and knowing no-one. We book into the YMCA. I know what you're thinking. Stop it. The Village People didn't release YMCA until 1978. We weren't comfortable in downtown Honolulu. Being the son of a policeman, Dad had been transferred around a bit and I had lived in Harvey, Brunswick, Donnybrook and Bunbury - all small country towns in Western Australia. Mick was originally from Northam, also a small country town. We were just a couple of country kids really. Honolulu felt like any other city, except for palm trees, Hawaiian shirts, Don Ho and the fact nearly every building was a tourist hotel. We did a quick tour of Oahu, I remember pineapples, lots of fucking pineapples, a disappointing Banzai Pipeline beach and an art exhibition at a remote hotel where they had an original Dali hanging. Salvador is following us around!

We wasted little time in finding the hydrofoil ferry to remote Maui, to get out of Honolulu. If Haight Ashbury was the epicentre of the hippie movement in 1968, then Maui was the last resort in May 1976. Within a few minutes we're sitting under a palm tree playing guitar and singing with "Seagull", a Robert Plant lookalike. He tells us to seek out Waianapanapa National Park, a remote camping spot near Hana, on the eastern tip of the island. Hitchhiking, we get picked up by a guy in a ute. We threw our backpacks and guitar in the back and it was 3 across the bench seat. Our driver passed us the chillum as soon as we got in ... Maui Wowie. The road to Hana has 617 hairpin bends, 59 one lane bridges and blind spots everywhere. It even has a little prayer grotto built into the lava jungle, ostensibly to protect drivers on their journey. Every now and again there's an abandoned car over the cliff edge. Our guy is totally off his tree! But it's ok because, by the third bend in the road, so are we. We loved that drive.

> *I spend about half an hour chatting with Lauren. She asks about Glen's nursing career, our family history, the farm, our business etc. I like the way she has raised Glen's arms a little to help with her fluid retention. I can already see skin folds whereas before, her skin was shiny and stretched. Lauren is working diligently and tells me Glen will be looked after by a different Debbie tonight. She also says she would trust her life with the new contestant. This is a big rap! ICP 11, BP 131/59. At 6.09pm Lauren and two beefy male assistants are ready to turn Glen and reposition her so, I offer to step out before they boot me out.*

Waianapanapa became home for our orange coloured 2-man tent, Mick and myself, plus my guitar. Whenever we walked to Hana, swam at the black sand beach, sat in the lava caves, or collected magic mushrooms, papayas and guavas, we would diligently secure the tent and the guitar. "Are you sure you've done the zip up?" "yes, all the way", "are you sure? ok we're good to go". Once, after a couple of mushrooms which "are having no effect on me at all", I suddenly realised I was swimming about 50 metres offshore. Pretty scary when you've just watched Jaws. One day after zipping the tent, we really did go – we left Waianapanapa, hitchhiking past Jaws surf break to Makena Beach in Kihei on the dry side of the island.

We'd heard good reports about Makena on the backpacker grapevine and, as soon as we met Gemstone, Rainbow and Eve on the nude beach, we knew we were in the right place. I learnt to play nude frisbee football on Makena. Mick learnt to make a quick dash to the water every time he started getting an inappropriate erection. Every morning from a rocky ridge, "Cowboy" from Idaho would welcome the sunrise ... nude, wearing only his cowboy boots. At night, 10-20 people would gather around a beach campfire for dinner. Mick used a rag for insulation when lifting the boiling hot tin of baked beans from the fire, only later sheepishly admitting he had burnt Jeanna Jellyroll's only item of clothing, a sari ... of sorts. We concluded it was inconsequential, as she didn't need a sari on a nude beach anyway. Jeanna was well known because she lived in a tree. Don't ask me how she lived in a tree but that's the truth. It just occurred to me that's probably why Jeanna owned the sari. It could get nasty up a tree in the nude, but I'm probably barking up the wrong tree. As usual, I would entertain around the campfire with Rainbow and two Canadians Peter and Richard. Pete was a drummer and Richard a bass player, both from Vancouver. I remember playing my first ever lead break around that campfire. I impressed myself that night, but it must have been the weed, because I'm still totally NOT a lead guitarist. We were invited to a house party in Kihei where we ascended a staircase to a room where about 10 musos sat around in a circle with guitars. I joined in as did Richard, who played the bottom 4 strings as a bass. I always smile when I recall Richard, fumbling for the right notes while an attractive young woman curled her tongue in his ear.

When Pete and Richard flew back to Vancouver they gave us a big brown paper bag full of dope ... enough to keep us going until we flew out for San Francisco a few days later. We spent our last night in

Maui at the Blue Max bar in Lahaina. We were hoping for a glimpse of the owner Stephen Stills, ex Crosby, Stills, Nash and Young. It wasn't to be, but we did receive a consolation prize – the backpacker grapevine was on fire that night with a rumour of free international phone calls to anywhere in the world. We followed a steady stream of hopeful itinerants to a street side public phone box, where a queue of about 20 people were lined up. As we eventually got to the head of the line, I asked the guy in front of me how it all worked? "Simple ... when they ask for your credit card number give them these 4 numbers, then just make up the next eight numbers, then finish with these other 4 numbers". So, I did. It worked, and I surprised my Mum with my first call home.

Helena Zynstein rented a beautiful old San Franciscan terrace house on Clipper Street in Noe Valley, just up the hill from Dolores Park in Mission and a quick walk to Buds Ice Cream, Castro and Diamond streets. Nowadays, it's a stone's throw from Silicon Valley. We'd become good friends around the campfire on Maui and, Helena had very kindly offered both of us a bed when we arrived in San Francisco. The "Death of the Hippie" mock funeral was Oct 6th 1967, but San Francisco was still an incredibly vibrant city in 1976. Dolores Park was full of artists, the most amazing buskers were on virtually every corner and we discovered that breakfast could be an event. We walked down Clipper to the corner, where a ballerina was busking in full tutu with a gentleman cello player dressed in black and white tux, joining Helena's friends for a morning of live music, coffee and a game of pool with our Spanish omelette. Something happened in my mind right then, I don't quite know what it was, but the whole cultural experience would work its way into a song of mine years later. The song was called Gerry Humphrys, named after the lead vocalist of The Loved Ones, a great innovative Australian band. If you've never heard of them listen to Ever Lovin' Man, The Loved One or Blueberry Hill. After San Francisco, I never slept in a tent again. Helena's brother-in-law was a roadie for Carlos Santana, so I listened intently to his stories and walked the pathways at Dolores Park where Santana was known to surprise with the occasionally busk. We were all invited next door for a party. By the time we arrived, there were trumpets, a clarinet, violins, guitars, a bass, drums and a female singer totally blowing my mind. This is all happening in the kitchen. A stranger walked in with a trombone and the conversation goes like this: "can I join in?" ... "can you read concert music?" ... "of course!". I left thinking everybody in San Francisco in 1976 read concert music ... except me. We spent about 3 weeks in Noe Valley before making the move to Vancouver, where our mate Pete from Maui, had offered us a roof over our head.

We intended going straight to Penticton to pick fruit, but Vancouver was irresistible. We lived in Pete's basement in Tanner street, Burnaby for a short time, where he had a full band rehearsal room. We were warm and cosy and it was exciting being immersed in the life of a full-time musician. I loved it. Pete would sleep during the day before waking early afternoon, for a solid practice session in the basement. His band, The Handley Page Group had recently busted up and he was auditioning for a new lead guitarist. The rehearsal songs were Pretzel Logic by Steely Dan and How Long by Ace. Being a fly on the wall, I thought every guy auditioning was fantastic, but Pete was very particular and demanding about the sound and level of professionalism he wanted. It was very interesting to me, watching the process. Today, both those songs are on my Spotify playlist. By now it's late May 1976 and after tropical Maui, Vancouver feels like the northern hemisphere summer in Poole, England.

I get called back into ICU. Glen is settled and the new contestant Debbie is busy. I talk softly into Glen's ear, words of comfort and encouragement, I hold her hand and tell her I'm going to rub her foot "probably your left foot". As I watch Debbie I feel Glen's left foot moving occasionally, I'm taking this as a good sign because this is supposedly going to be her deficit side. She looks calm. ICP 11, BP 130/62. Debbie switches IV drips, repositions Glen's arm. Glen moves her left foot again. The intercom has requested all visitors leave so I won't watch Debbie work all night, but she could be challenging the leader board here. Other nurses are asking her questions and she answers with authority and confidence, while still busying herself looking after Glen. As I rub her foot I know she is in good hands. Debbie is definitely catching up to Brooke here. OMG she's even got the calculator out! Glen gives me a friendly lift of the left foot.

Mick and I totally fail at strawberry picking on the outskirts of Vancouver. Then we totally fail again, as car detailers. We were still partying hard and, when you're getting paid piecemeal to detail cars, it pays to get to work really early to claim the small cars like the Pintos and small sedans. Rocking up with a hangover at 8am gets you the big Oldsmobile, the big Buick and the big Cadillac. One thing though, we were fast learners. We quit on the second day! I can't recall the Pakistani owner even paying us to be honest. We knew our strength, and it wasn't detailing cars. Richard introduced us to Gerd Imhoff, a Canadian businessman of German descent. I was totally unaware Gerd would have a profound impact on my life.

This is getting very tight, Debbie is all over it. She's sucking mouth fluid, rubbing lip cream, wiping Glen's eyes, checking cannulas, sanitising her hands, gloves on - gloves off, rearranging arm supports, entering data points ... all the while answering questions from other nurses. I'm calling a progress score ... it's a draw. If Glen gets up and walks I'm giving it to Debbie! Propofol is still on 50, ICP at 12 and BP is 127/62. Debbie hasn't asked, but lately they've been keen for me to leave by about now so I pre-empt the inevitable. By 9.00pm 24th May, the warm sunny days we shared with Glen at Cottesloe prior to her first surgery are a distant memory. I realise what I've just said. How easy is it for me to dismiss a memory as inconsequential? When Glen wakes up, I desperately want her to be able to remember those few days. The Nedlands puddles are everywhere as I trudge to the car park. I think of earlier today, squinting through the windscreen wipers, through the misty blur of the leafy western suburbs to find the grey monocoloured sameness of a Donnybrook winter. It feels like winter. I hate the thought that my girl Glen is going to wake up in a different season. I buy a carton of Peroni on the way home even though I know Mick will protest because he owns a liquor store. We share a quiet beer, before I retire and practice my meditation and prayer for 30 minutes, before falling into a deep sleep.

Tues 25th May

I wake at 4.56am feeling rejuvenated and Pete has sent me another overnight message of encouragement from Vancouver. Even Bitcoin is fighting hard. After the obligatory shower and shave I'm out the door by 6.40am only to be disappointed la Galette is still closed. I opt for scrambled eggs, tomato, bacon, toast and a flat white at Cafe Bourbar opposite. By 7.30am I'm seated below the ICU waiting room handset and I text the kids to let them know all is well. I'm not allowed in yet.

We began as gardeners, attending to Gerd's multistorey residential apartment block in Kitsilano, Vancouver. We knew nothing about gardening but, we must have impressed as Gerd promoted us to be janitors - another field of expertise we knew nothing about. Gerd moved us into warehouse assistant roles for his burgeoning umbrella importing business. Mick became adept at fixing broken umbrellas, order compilation, despatch, stocktake, storage and movement, basically running the entire warehouse. I was promoted into the office, keeping the daily books up to date, liaising with Dennis Shikaze his accountant, and eventually becoming Gerd's Office Manager whenever he was away in Taiwan, Montreal or Germany. Occasionally, of an evening, either Gerd or his wife Christine would ask if I could babysit their daughters Stephanie and Tanja. Vancouver is a beautiful city, fringed by snow-capped mountains to the north and dissected by the snaking Fraser River. The Lions Gate bridge hangs like a mini Golden Gate over the final delta, linking North Vancouver to Stanley Park. A ferry ride from downtown takes city workers to the foot of Grouse Mountain, where a chair lift has them skiing the slopes within 30 minutes of knocking off work. Stanley Park itself is a magnificent 1,000-acre forest of autumn colour, summer fun and natural beauty. The pathway around the perimeter, the Seawall, would in time become my jogging circuit. Pete knew every nightclub, pub, restaurant and cafe around Granville. All I needed was my body shirt, black crushed velvet jumpsuit, full-length leather coat and platform shoes from the Black Sheep boutique in Gastown and I was on fire.

Mick and I had moved into a share house in Union St. Burnaby, a short drive down Boundary Road and not too far from Pete's basement. Our housemates Brenda and Joanne had a decent stereo and we were listening to Frampton Comes Alive and George Benson's Breezin' on vinyl rotation, loud. We were still partying hard in various Vancouver clubs and Pete was doing the odd cameo gig with Zingo and his ex Handley Page guitarist Keith Scott, nowadays guitarist for Bryan Adams. Pete would take us salmon mooching out of Horseshoe Bay. Towing his Dads tiny tinnie through the dark, we would arrive pre-dawn, buy our live bait pilchards on the wharf then quietly cut our way across the glass, winding north around the shoreline with the rail line carved into the mountainside above us. Sometime in early August 1976, we sat outside in the sunshine and shared a meal with our housemate Brenda's family. It's funny the things you remember ... the table was set up on the lawn in the back garden with a multi coloured tablecloth, the turkey, the water melon, the dog. It was a bit like home in a way, in the company of her brother and parents. Mick speaks of skateboarding with her brother in the driveway, and the drive as we approached her parents' house, north out of Vancouver, thru the never-ending forest until we emerged at an amazing pristine lake. I wish I could remember that!

We were both loving life in Vancouver. We were settling in. Mick and I were planning on buying a second-hand Corvette for $11,000 and we were living one day at a time ... just like I'm doing right now at Glen's bedside. Within a week, Mick was deported. Arrested on a Friday, they kept him in custody all weekend, a quick court case on Monday, then 2 days to get out of the country. We were both working while on non-working holiday visas. He was arrested in the umbrella warehouse by 2 guys wearing dark suits. Immigration officers. As I glance up from my desk I caught their purposeful walk past the office window. I knew something was wrong. They gave him a choice: (a) pay your own way back home to Australia and you will be allowed back into Canada or, (b) the Canadian Govt. pays your airfare out, but you will never be allowed back into Canada again. Mick asked them one question, "Where are you going to send me?" "Anywhere" they said. Mick was in London just in time to catch the free Queen concert in Hyde Park on 18th Sept 1976.

Run Steve, Run

I was devastated, lost, and a bit scared for my own situation in the aftermath of Mick's arrest as I was on the same holiday visa, working at the same business. Feeling alone and, with a renewed sense of apprehension, I started running. Actually, really, running. I ran, and ran, and ran. Looking back on it now, I did a mini Tom Hanks/ Forest Gump. I started by jogging Adanac Park, a small soccer field at the bottom of Union Street before progressing to running the suburbs after work in the dark. Never having been into exercise, I threw myself into pre-dawn runs in the Vancouver rain, sometimes running with a head torch past the crazy fly fishermen practicing their cast into a roadside lake. My life changed in so many ways in Vancouver, it's hard to know where to begin. Overnight, I became a vegetarian, well ... sort of. I gave up eating all things red meat. Fish, chicken, cheese and eggs were still in. Cutting red meat was not a crusade to save animals, simply a means of disciplining myself to have conviction and trust in my own decisions. I felt a renewed urgency to find a way where I could believe in myself, I felt it was me versus the rest of the world. For the first time since 6th June 1974, I was truly alone. I needed to prepare my mind and body to be ready for whatever opportunities came my way. Strengthening my resolve was a start. I traded my hippie clothes for a 3-piece suit. Keith Richards must have liked the same suit, he bought one for his

Toronto court appearance in March 1977. I cut my hair. I wrote my first real song. I was running. It was about this time I wrote a letter to Glen, addressed c/- Post Restante Madrid, as I knew she was travelling Europe with her cousin Phill, his wife Judy, her best friend Steph and partner Grant, and another guy called Gerry who, at the time was Glen's boyfriend. I was really missing her, and wanted her to know how I felt. It was in Vancouver that I began to realise I was in love with Glen. Months and years later she would confess to me that the Post Restante letter threw doubt into her mind and her relationship with Gerry, and this is probably the genesis of what I believe is a beautiful love story, the best story of my life and, a long and winding road that would lead to Glen's bedside as I write.

It was exciting being mentored in business and I was inspired working with Gerd. We would talk into the night about business, franchise plans, expansion and major dept store marketing programs. Driving around Vancouver I didn't hesitate to call into smaller outlets, chat to managers, introduce new lines. Gerd gave me use of his green Pontiac, my C$80 Ford (with the wooden 3 ply fly window) wasn't good enough. Harry the salesman would come into the office looking like Pierce Brosnan, and I just knew I could move more umbrellas than him. Gerd offered me an opportunity to establish and operate a new Quebec office.

> *8.48am I've been waiting long enough so it's handset time again ... "yes, you can come through". I reckon they forgot about me. I'm a bit annoyed but relieved to see Glen stable and the new contestant Dee assures me everything is ok. ICP 10, BP 119/60, Propofol set at 50. Dee says she'll be back after her tea break ... but that move just cost her points on the tally board. Kaylee is back as an intruder trying to score a few random votes but doctors intervene*

and ask me to step outside again before she gets a vote. The ICU waiting room is a great leveller. In between the tears and the tension, everyone knows we are all in the same boat, in the same storm, on the same daily roller coaster, hanging for the next move forward or, slumping in despair on the next bad news. A young man is pacing, anxious, he's new to the waiting room but his eyes are already bloodshot. When he's alone I put my hand on his shoulder and try to comfort him a little ... "you know these guys are miracle workers in here ... every single day they perform miracles, keep your chin up mate and good luck". Dr Brad comes into the corridor and motions me inside. No waiting room call on the handset? I'm worried but he calms me immediately as we walk inside. They've cut the sedation (Propofol) to 0 and the Fentanyl (painkiller) to 0. Pressures are good, BP good ... they are expecting no real change today but will now be looking for more reactive responses as time passes. Dylan arrives and sends Hannah a text as Dee tests for stimulus response: "Mums off the Propofol at the moment. ICP - 8, BP- 140/71, Heart rate – 104. Ventilator is still in but she's breathing fully on her own at the moment. Reaction to painful stimuli on all limbs - this indicates no permanent loss of movement (so far). No purposeful movements on the left arm - but the left arm and shoulder are shrugging a lot. Still sleeping. The nurse Dee is great." I'm feeling nervous about claiming "this indicates no permanent loss of movement (so far)", too many roller coasters here, touch wood. Dylan insists. I ask Dee how do you know if she may be in discomfort? Dee says "Dylan is pretty switched on isn't he ... he asked about her data numbers and resting on the right side (the op side) of her head, it was time for a turn". 11.05am Dee presses a pen lightly against Glen's fingernails and toenails ... testing for withdrawal movement. All 4 limbs react. Dylan might be on to something ... I'm feeling positive. We just want her to wake up now.

We call Brad over again and he pulls Glen's last scan up on the monitor. We can see the brain damage on the right side. It's quite extensive. He goes on to explain the scans are useful but "crude", in the sense they can indicate possible effects to certain known control areas of the brain ... but ultimately, they won't really know the extent of any damage until Glen wakes up. He says sometimes people wake up with better function than the scan indicated, other times it is the opposite. He does however, confirm my fears that Glen has more than likely lost function in her left arm and, will suffer some deficit in the left leg. We are hopeful that with rehab, her left leg can re learn to maybe function fully again. Of course, all of this is conjecture until she wakes up. The other field of deficit is predicted to be her abstract thinking, like dressing herself, cooking, calculating etc.
One day at a time, one hurdle at a time. We can do this. Dee is good, a dark horse? 11.35am and it's "turn Glen time". We decide it's Steve's pub in Nedlands for an early lunch, before Hannah and I take the first of the afternoon shifts sitting with Glen. When the boys rock up they all decide I should go for a rest. I don't argue. I crashed about 3pm before waking at 5.45pm. I'm on the road back to ICU at 6pm. Our new nurse is named Pepita, I've just been allowed back in. Think they forgot about me again, I had to ask. ICP is 6, BP 125/68. Propofol 50. All good. I call it a day at 9.00pm. It's easy to lose the days and dates in

ICU ... I check and it's 9.00am 26th May 2021. It's now 2 months since Glen had the stent op. How our world has changed. The young man with the bloodshot eyes comes over and thanks me profusely. He says my few words made "all the difference". He introduces himself as David, named after his 55-year-old father who is lying in the bed next to Glen. After a massive stroke they are waiting on his scans this morning before a meeting with the doctors. By 9.15 I'm back in and the new contestant is named Aimee. It's getting very tight in the middle of the leader board, but at this stage it's still Brooke on top with Tarah bringing up the rear. Please don't take offence Tarah, I realise you do a wonderful job every day, you just got me on my bad day. I text the kids: "I'm in with Mum now ... she looks gr8 ... they've taken the dressing off and the stitches are visible. ICP 7, BP 127/60. Breathing ok 7.7"

By now I'd learnt on the backpacker grapevine that I could get all my tax back. I was making about C$1,000 a week which was more money than I'd ever made in my life and I'd paid a lot of tax. I'm told to go to the central post office and apply for a social security number using some false data. I study a map of Canada to pick my new birthplace. Swift Current, Saskatchewan - it's the most remote place I can find. I tell them I was a homebirth, no hospital records. I feel like an Inuit already! Maybe I'll get an extra allowance? As the Vancouver winter sets in, I'm running more and more in the dark. Still wary of the Canadian Dept of Immigration and knowing my visa will run out in May, I tell Gerd I'm heading to Mexico for Christmas. "No problems, take as long as you like - the job is here when you return." Gerd has already talked about sponsoring me as an immigrant and I'm planning an exciting future.

At 10.40am Hannah and I are booted out while they turn Glen and attend to their "secret duties." Nothing sinister, I'm sure, it just makes life easier if visitors are not around. My mind is a confusion of in ICU, out ICU, in, out, in out. David comes over and offers me some home-made biscuits, it's a strange bond between total strangers, close ... but far.

I tell Brenda and Joanne about my Mexico plans and we agree it's best for them to advertise for a new tenant as Richard has offered to rent me a room in his house upon my return. Canada Umbrella shuts for the Christmas break, just in time for Pete to score me a few day's work stocktaking at Kenworth trucks. More bucks! We look forward to lunch times when the stainless-steel mobile food van delivers the usual crappy food and Pete practices his drumming on a small portable pad while I befriend Austen, an African Canadian guy. Austen took us to a couple of great downtown clubs where Tower of Power lit up the dance pit with There Ain't Nothin' Stoppin' Us Now.

By now I have accumulated "a bit of stuff". I pack it all into my new chestnut brown leather suitcase, backpack long gone. I'm wearing my Keith Richards 3-piece suit, with matching full-length leather coat, carrying my guitar. I'm not proud of the arctic wolf fur collar. I leave winter in Vancouver for the sunshine in Puerto Vallarta, Mexico on December 22nd 1976, coincidentally Glen's birthday. As the cabin door opens it's about 95 degrees Fahrenheit. I knew I was going to be overdressed but not this overdressed! I drive my pre-booked vee dub convertible to the best hotel in town, made famous by Elizabeth Taylor and Richard Burton in Night of the Iguana. The valet parking attendant thinks I'm a rock star and asks if I'll perform in the bar that night. Everything is smoke and mirrors, if you can't play, at least look like you can. The ultimate poseur. In hindsight, I should have said yes, but I didn't.

2.09pm kicked out for physio. 3 boys back in the waiting room but it's a short break before Jake and I re-enter. George, the ICU neuro Doctor comes over and the bottom line is, it's important for Glen to be off the ventilator within 3-4 days or they may have to do a tracheotomy. Shattered again. The poor bastard has a tough job, he delivers this news with the usual platitudes and sombre demeanour, but we know he's softening us up if there's no improvement. I shed a tear when "Humpty Dumpty" comes to mind but I quickly dispel any negativity. I hate this fucking roller coaster. We check out early, only because I've organised to have dinner at Hannah's with the family. I text Mick, let him know, and battle the traffic to Embleton. Hannah cooks a delicious chicken dish with noodles and Asian vegetables. When I see the sambal oelek on the side I am reminded of Glen's father Johan, or Joop as we called him. He was born in Sumatra to Dutch Indonesian parents. During the Sukarno led uprising against the Dutch colonialists, Joop's family fled Padangpanjang as the bridge behind their train was detonated and destroyed. Joop was 16 years of age. He was seconded into the Dutch navy submarines, without the opportunity of saying goodbye to his parents. He never saw them again. Joop married Eleanor Patterson (Nel) in Perth at the conclusion of WW11 and Glen's Mum became a genius in the kitchen. Sambal oelek was always on her table and always in our pantry.

Thurs 27th May

I finally get in at 11.23am and immediately text the kids: "ICP was taken out late yesterday. No Propofol since we saw her yesterday apparently. No adrenaline since midnight, just 1 ml/hr fentanyl. Moving her right arm a bit.

I spoke to her and told her all about dinner last night etc, and her BP went up to 170 while I was speaking, also her right arm was moving at that time and her face reddened a bit. I reckon she could hear me. Still asleep looks calm, pillow positioned to keep her feet straight and pushed backwards a bit. All good. Holding her hand now". I've decided to call ICU Nurse, the reality show result. It's too confusing remembering everyone so, I'm giving it to (drum roll) ... Brooke! Debbie gets a special mention and is encouraged to enter again next year as it was incredibly tight. If Rodger was an ICU nurse I reckon he would have taken it out but his gig is HDU - High Dependency Unit. Hopefully that's where Glen will be in a few days. If he wins there, he definitely scores the grand prize of a potential trip to Abrolhos islands. Nurse Mel shines a torch into each of Glen's eyes and the left pupil response is strong. It's been ok all along. Her right pupil is not responding.

It's a 271-kilometre drive from Puerto Vallarta south to Manzanillo and about a 4.5-hour drive in the banana yellow convertible Beetle. Tom Hunt and his girlfriend Wendy are in an apartment in Las Brisas there, and I'd arranged to rent with them. Wearing boardies, T shirt and thongs I get an early start ... guitar in the passenger seat, suitcase and rock star costume in the back. Right now, I realise time is so precious, I won't dwell on every little detail of my travels. I'm going to distil my 3 months in Mexico into a few clear memories. It's Christmas Eve 1976 and we are in the Manzanillo Town Square, watching the locals dance to the Mariachi band. Felice Navidad by Jose Feliciano and Guantanamera seem to be on permanent rotation. Tacos, cerveza and cerviche are all on the menu in the nearby Cantina. After a week or two, I feel like the richest guy in town and it dawns on me that real wealth is ... time. The real purpose of life is to pursue our passion and express our true purpose, but I'm confused about what my true purpose is. I throw myself into guitar and singing and trying to write songs then, one night I have this weird "out of body" sort of experience, where my left hand is no longer mine. I'm not in control and I'm watching it move around the neck of the guitar. I start to write a song but it dies as a riff, I'm trying too hard and it's pointless forcing a song. The baby doesn't get born until it's fully developed.

I get frustrated in my lack of progress so, I decide I'll become an author instead. Simple. I hand write 2 pages of total crap before I realise it's the worst story I've ever read. Not a problem, I'll become an artist! I'll paint watercolours. The guy in the Manzanillo art shop must have thought all his navidads had come at once when I spent a small fortune on all the gear - easel, paints, brushes, papers, knife, palette etc. As I'm setting up on the beach to paint the scene across the bay to the town itself, a small crowd of local kids begins to assemble. You know the rest ... my daubs and splashes are an absolute disaster, the kids giggle, I'm so embarrassed I pack up and leave. I should have donated all that stuff to the kids, maybe I did, I can't remember. So, I give up on finding the passion, but I keep singing and playing nonetheless. Later in life I would come to the realisation that it's not necessarily about the passion, but it is all about never giving up. 25 years later, when our daughter was leaving Australia on her own backpacker journey, her boyfriend Kade came to me and asked, "Steve, can you write a going away song for Hannah?" I was partying and in my drunken bravado agreed to the challenge. Musically I had nothing, but I'd never forgotten the stillborn 1977 Mexican riff and, I'd learnt a few new chords since then. Still, I was bereft of inspiration, so I hand-balled it to my son Jake, with no instructions. He came back within a few days, turning what I thought was the verse into the chorus, and the whole song suddenly made musical sense. I rewrote the verse, added a bridge and it became "Hannah's Song". Jake and I recorded it at home in STEM studios Donnybrook, and Kade, who she eventually married, did a fantastic job of mixing and producing the song. Hannah took the CD with her to London and I like to think maybe, just maybe, it was heard by Paul McCartney who she met through her work. I doubt it, but who knows! The outro features the beautiful speaking voices of both her grandmothers, and in retrospect, the song captured a beautiful moment in all our lives.

Tom and I bought a speargun and we began snorkelling every day, catching whatever fish we needed for meals. We became so good at it, we began taking orders from the guy next door for certain eating species. He owned the adjacent Tienda de Licores, or liquor store. We traded fish for booze ... cerveza (beer) and tequila. We were then approached by his mates, a farmer and the local milko, so it was free booze, bananas, capsicums cucumbers and milk. Tom was so flat broke he sold his blood to raise some cash, I went with him, but wasn't tempted. With only one speargun, we would take turns fishing. Once, I was sitting on a rock when Tom was surprised by a gray whale in quite shallow water. I thought it was hilarious as the scene unfolded in slow motion and Tom shat himself. We preferred to fish in a little bay just behind and to the north of Las Hadas, the hotel where Bo Derek and Dudley Moore filmed the movie 10.

Glen worked night shift with Mary Brown for 17 years. Together, they formed part of a close team of midwives working at St John of God Hospital in Bunbury, Western Australia, under the guidance and management of Sister Killian. Mary's husband Alistair, also a nurse and eventually Nurse Manager there, knew them all. Mary and Alistair arrive to visit Glen in ICU just as I finish a bedside chat with Prof Lind. Again, Lind renewed my hope so I immediately text the kids: "Just had a chat with Prof Chris Lind at the foot of Mum's bed. He is "very positive and optimistic" that Mum will wake up. Not sure when ... all depends on how quick the swelling goes down. He is happy with how everything is tracking. I asked him about the tracheotomy ... he said he does not see it as a "retrograde step". He said it may be required in ~3 days to prevent risk of pneumonia and damage to vocal chords. He is confident that if necessary it is the right thing to do. He says the op is reversible when possible. Very standard op apparently. I feel a lot better after that conversation. Of course, the perfect scenario is swelling goes down and Mum wakes up. All good ... Mary and Alistair visited ... I'm having dinner with them now. Onwards and upwards"

We drive to Northbridge, meet Mary's nursing friend Sue, then stroll about 50 metres to Vincents for a shared meal and a glass of Chardonnay. The three healthcare workers further help allay my fears regarding the possible tracheotomy, before Mary and Alistair fly out to Queensland at midnight. I'm back at Mick's, asleep by 11pm.

Fri 28th May

7.21am I immediately check my phone on waking, there is a text from Hannah: "A very proud big sister ... happy that her little brother got his first tooth" I'm feeling good today, today will be a good day. By 9.15am I'm at Glen's bedside and text the kids: "I'm in with Mum now ... new nurse Allanah assured me Glen was stable overnight. Apparently, it was perfect timing as they just finished washing her. Mum looks good, resting and calm. Am I imagining it or *has the facial swelling gone down a bit? It looks better to me. Allanah says localised right arm and leg movements continuing, with some movement (more reflexive) in left leg. No movement in left arm. No different from yesterday. All data points are good. No Propofol ... but still on low 1 ml/hr fentanyl pain killer. I asked nurse why has NORAD (adrenaline) been increased to 6.03 ml/hr, she says ... we don't want her to "dry out" too much, the adrenaline helps move the fluid around within the body ... anyway all good I'm sitting here now."*

Sometimes, if we were feeling brave enough to trust the driver, we'd take the rickety yellow public transport bus from Las Brisas into town and traverse the hill overlooking Manzanillo. The walk trail started opposite the busy Tortilleria at street level, then wound its way up past the haciendas splattered across the hillside. We never saw any other westerners on the hill, two gringos were an oddity, and the little muchachos followed us like we were the Pied Piper. Often, in the midday heat we'd occasionally rest on a verandah overlooking the town and buy a coke. Every home had a fridge on the verandah and every house was a coke shop. We'd usually shout one or two of the kids a coke, hence our popularity. We always looked forward to reaching the summit of Town Hill, because from that height we could tell immediately how clear the water at Town Beach would be. If the visibility was special, snorkelling was so much more fun and relaxing, and we could spot marine life we wouldn't always see.

Nowadays, Manzanillo calls itself the sailfish capital of the world, but the only one I saw was draped unceremoniously sideways, across a small aluminium dinghy. It's a vision that has stayed with me through the years and today, I practice catch and release whenever I can, only taking fish I know are for the table. We swam with a variety of species including mahi mahi or dorado as the locals called it, barracuda, goatfish, dart, giant trevally and massive schools of baitfish. There was always a few muchachos on the beach, watching us and, it wasn't long before my Spanish vocabulary was good enough to converse, albeit spoken in a Hollywood movie accent. My childhood memories of the Cisco Kid were invaluable. Unfortunately, some of these kids were addicted to sniffing glue from a plastic bag, Resistol 5000 was their drug of choice. A very sad situation. I can still see young Jorge's yellow stained face, bloodshot eyes and vacant stare. I just hope he found a life, it was up to him, but his future did not look bright. Occasionally, we'd lend the spearfishing gear and the local boys would take home a feed. When we needed to go home we simply yelled "tiburones", and waved our arms, pointing ... they soon came in.

Sitting on the Town Beach sand, looking over a glass-out on a perfect day, I saw something weird across the bay. I could see a splash, glinting in the sunshine as it moved in a straight line toward me. The splashes were perfectly equidistant and in perfect synchronicity. As the phenomenon got closer, I stood up and walked to the water's edge. I was actually a little nervous as I'd never seen anything like it, and it felt almost supernatural. As it came closer I realised it was a school of fish. Small, probably about 15cm long and silver, the fish leapt in perfect harmony and unison, in perfect rainbow formation. Leap, disappear, leap, disappear ... getting closer all the time in a straight line directly toward me. I thought they would jump right onto the sand at my feet then, in a few centimetres of water, they just disappeared, forever. Years later, Tim Winton would write something along the lines of ... "if you stare at the ocean long enough, it will offer up a gift". He's right, of course. I reckon he stole that line from me, I just hadn't written it yet.

Tom and I met Gerry Moody and his partner Mary Rose - Moody at the opening of his new cantina taco bar called the Taco Swap. He was an ex Vietnam vet and they were renting a large house overlooking Las Hadas. We'd often party on their flat rooftop where they had a bar and a couple of telescopes set up. My guitar was an entré to meeting many wonderful and interesting people during my travels ... but Gerry was an emotionally troubled man. Mary told me he had made his money smuggling cocaine from Central America into the US. Nowadays, I am sure he would be diagnosed with Post-Traumatic Stress Disorder. Anyway, one-night Gerry jumps in his own convertible VW beetle and tries to kill himself. Using the hand brake, he deliberately rolled the vehicle at high speed on the straight road between Las Hadas and Manzanillo itself. I visited him in hospital, if you can call it a hospital ... graffiti walls, bare concrete floor, dirty linen on a steel frame single bed, with Gerry looking like a mummy in traction. He never spoke, never moved, never acknowledged anyone's presence. They chartered a plane and flew him to Cedars Sinai Hospital in California. The rumour was they'd packed the plaster casts with cocaine but, to my knowledge, the story was never substantiated. Wendy had flown back to England already, so it was Tom and I hitchhiking out of Manzanillo in late March 1977. We made our way north to Puerto Vallarta, before catching the ferry to Cabo San Lucas. The ferry travelled all through the night and we sat on the deck drinking cerveza with a young Mexican couple. He had a guitar also, and we played Cielito Lindo for about an hour. Magic.

I'm out for physio, then in again. Hannah arrives, then upon leaving sends out this (long) text: "Just home from visiting Mum... she was looking peaceful and calm, I feel like she looks a little more 'like herself' today which is comforting. I saw her right eyelid twitch, most likely a reflex/involuntary - but I haven't seen that eyelid move AT ALL since after the initial stent procedure. Also, some right arm movements, that seemed to coincide with points of conversation, so I'm hopeful they were purposeful. I'm feeling a new sense of hope and positive vibes since Dad spoke with Dr Lind (head neurosurgeon) last night. Dad said he still seems very confident that Mum will wake, once the swelling reduces - but it will take time and no one can say how much time. I also quizzed the nurse this morning about whether they get a lot of long-term ventilated patients and she said yeah, all the time, very common. My professional brain knew this but it gets clouded when it's someone you love as opposed to being at work. I think although each stable day is a step in the right direction ... when nothing much changes day by day I had started to get nervous and doubt the process, feel impatient! Also feeling more at ease about the possibility of a tracheotomy. I've now had a chance to process the idea of Mum enduring another procedure, and knowing that it will be much more comfortable for her and that a lot of the time patients are ready for them to be reversed before leaving the ICU (obviously not always). So once again I have taken a deep breath and reminded myself that we have all the time in the world to wait until she is ready ... and to just take comfort in the fact that her body is recovering while she sleeps. This sure is a serious lesson in patience". Glen's brother Charlie lives in Perth so I call his wife Shirley and ask if they would like to visit Glen. They jump at the opportunity and I arrange to meet them in the ICU waiting room at 3pm.

We disembarked at Cabo San Lucas and began hitchhiking immediately, figuring we might be lucky enough to catch a ride with one of the vehicles as they drove off the ferry. We were right. A middle-aged couple in a sedan offered us a lift all the way up Baja California Peninsula to Tijuana. The ride became uncomfortable when we realised the wife in the passenger seat was totally intoxicated and verbally abusing her driver husband. Turns out he is the stand in for a famous Hollywood actor - Richard Widmark. She was tearing strips off this poor guy and he never said a word. "Do you know who this guy is? he's a fucking nobody, an absolute nobody, he's just a stand in, he'll never amount to anything", she snarls at him "you'll never be an actor". I looked at him from the back seat, yep it's Richard Widmark ... almost. "You're not Richard Widmark! You can't even wipe Richard Widmark's arse" she said. Tom and I just looked each other and hardly said a word the whole way to Tijuana.

Sat 29th May

Last night I caught up with Stewie at the Albion hotel in Cottesloe. Like me, he is so grateful for the support he is receiving from Mick, Spider, Homer and all the other backpackers we met all those years ago. Most of us are old and grey now, we've all known each other through the wild days, the glory days and the tough years too. There is a beautiful bond between us all. At 8.36pm I get a call on my phone, it's the unknown number. I panic and step outside, onto the pavement and into the rain for some privacy. It's Rodger, bless his soul, inquiring how Glen is and how we are all coping. I relax and have a couple more beers before leaving my car at the Albion and catching a lift home with Mick. I'm at Glen's bedside around 8.30am. Glen is quite active this morning, moving her right arm and leg frequently, also twitching both eyes slightly. Excitedly, I text the kids: "I'm with Mum now ... no change. Comfortable, nurse is a guy named Connor. Wow, I can't believe what just happened ... Connor tested her pupil reaction and her left pupil was good as usual but it was quite a strong response, and then the eyelid stayed open (about half way), and at the same time she moved her right hand. I saw her right eyelid twitch as well. Good signs xx". Dylan arrives early and while he's here Glen starts showing off with small but purposeful right arm and leg movements, as well as semi opening her left eyelid of her own accord. Both eyes are occasionally twitching simultaneously. These are the best signs we have had that Glen may be waking up. Hannah arrives with a card and news of a huge hamper from all the Bunbury girls. Like me with my old backpacker mates, Glen has a magnificent army of ex workmate friends and supporters praying and wishing her well. I just know she will pull through this. I've sucked and scavenged every ounce of energy from every person I know ... and I know this girl is a gladiator.

Another Saturday gone - I have dinner with all the kids at Hannah's and we watch the Eagles lose to Essendon by 16 points. The huge hamper from all Glen's nursing workmates in Bunbury sits on Hannah's table. I take a pic and send out a text before I drive back to Micks: "Some good news today folks. Glen is showing the earliest signs of recovery/waking up. We don't want to sound too optimistic at this early stage but ... Glen moved her right toes on demand today. The scans are saying her right leg/foot should be ok but to do it on demand means she understood the request and her state of consciousness is improving. Her left pupil response *has been ok all along but today I thought it was stronger and we saw tiny twitching of both eyes simultaneously ... once. We're feeling encouraged. First signs - big day today. Glen's colour is good, her BP pulse etc. all within acceptable parameters, her temperature good. I'm still expecting the tracheotomy to go in Monday morning though unless we have a massive day tomorrow. She's a fighter. Today we received a massive hamper from all Glen's amazing ex workmates in Bunbury. I can't thank you all enough for your prayers and support, I just know it's working. I know we are winning, but we are trying to keep a lid on our expectations here because until Glen wakes up we will not know the extent of her deficits."*

For years, I've jokingly called Glen superwoman. Superwoman for working night shift as a midwife while being a magnificent mother to three children, all the while simultaneously working in and co-managing a farm café/tearoom. Superwoman for her tears every Mother's Day, when she was grinding away in the tearoom commercial kitchen, when all the other mothers were being spoilt by their kids and, superwoman for simultaneously starting and operating a carpet cleaning business. Superwoman for nursing her mother Nel, her father Joop, my brother's wife Fran, my father Murray, my mother Pam and my uncle Rev ... supporting them all through their last months and days. Superwoman for being such a wonderful surrogate Nanna and Aunty Glen to Fran's grandchildren Marcie and Caris. Superwoman for being my travel agent, secretary, teacher, housekeeper and biggest fan and, superwoman for working every New Year's Eve while I was gigging. I've had a great lifetime of playing and singing but, without Glen's ears, I'm sure I'd give it away. Finally, superwoman for being the most amazing wife, lover and soulmate to me, her husband, who has never changed a nappy in his life.

Sun 30th May

8.00am. After the excitement of yesterday's tentative signs of waking I'm in early. Lauren, our Bunbury contestant, tells me there is no change and Glen is wiggling her right toes on request. Her eyes are closed, but Glen looks good and I'm telling myself the swelling has gone down even more since yesterday. Jake and Tegan come, then swap with Dylan. I continue tapping away with one finger, much to Dylan's chagrin, it frustrates the shit out of him.

If I never see Tijuana again I don't care. After three fantastic months in Mexico, I eat tacos from a street vendor on the last day, and so begins a downward spiral of Montezuma's Revenge that would span the whole west coast of America. Tom and I catch a bus to San Diego where we sign up with Nationwide Auto. We're to deliver a car from San Diego to Portland, Oregon for a used car dealership. They supply the car, fuel and insurance, we supply the time, labour and our own accommodation. We're thinking a Cadillac Convertible, T Bird or maybe a Corvette. They bring it out, it's a Datsun 180B ... fuck. They gave us four days to complete the journey, but we figure if we boot it we could do a bit of sightseeing along the way. We've now got the fastest Datsun 180B on the whole west coast of America. Most of the time I'm prostrate in the back seat, groaning with stomach cramps. Just outside of Bakersfield, Tom is exhausted and I have to drive. I've got the Datsun absolutely flat to the floor, concentrating between stomach cramps, not looking at the speedometer. Suddenly, a police car comes at us heading in the opposite direction. I figure I'm going so fast I can outrun him. I keep going. The 180B is shaking like shit but performing like a beauty, there's no police car in the rear-view mirror so I'm feeling smug, really smug, until I see the flashing lights up ahead. As I get closer, there is a police car parked sideways blocking the road, and the Sheriff is standing front and centre, gun drawn, both hands aimed directly at me. I think he scared Montezuma's shit right out of me. He's a big guy, full uniform, hat, reflective sunnies, badge, but I'm really only seeing the gun. It's all a bit of a blur here really ... I seriously thought I could talk my way out of it, like I'd done so many times back in Oz. I tried my best "I'm the son of a policeman" story, that didn't work. I pleaded the "I'm on an international passport" excuse, I figured the bureaucratic paperwork would be too much for him, that didn't work either. Finally, I told him we were leaving the US for Canada in two days. I'm not sure if any of those ploys worked, but I felt smug again, driving away with just a US$40 fine.

Sun 30th May

2.10pm. Jake has gone into town for a catch up with some Roy Hill workmates and Dylan has gone for lunch with his mate Rob and his wife Harriet. Since the decompression craniectomy, all Glen's data points have stabilised, it's a huge relief and I find I'm not watching them continuously. We are watching intently for indications the swelling is reducing and hopefully signs of waking.

By the time I return to Vancouver the worst of winter has passed and I'm renting a room in Richard's house. I'm running, listening to The Eagles' *Hotel California* album and Paul Simon's *Still Crazy After All These Years*. Richard and I are running the suburbs nightly, and the 10-kilometre Stanley Park Seawall is an easy run every weekend. I'm back at Canada Umbrella with Gerd but manage a sojourn with Richard, through the Rockies to Jasper, Banff and the Columbia Icefields. Gerd and Christine invite me up to the Sunshine Coast for a few days in their friend Peter's cottage. We take a seaplane to Sechelt, then snake through the forest in a hire car as we follow the glassy waters of the inland passage. This becomes a magical time exploring the wilderness and the dark, tannin waters of the tiny fishing village of Lund, as well as mooching and actually catching a salmon in Peter's little zodiac dinghy. The cedar cabin was really about three cabins on three levels down to the water's edge, where every morning a family of seals would perform and greet us with their raucous honking. Inside, huge marine ropes hung a bookshelf from the ceiling, and a massive block of cedar stood as an island work bench in the kitchen. The cabin was complete with a huge log fireplace, red wine and the warm vinyl tones of Joni Mitchell and Carol King. To this day, I still love listening to a good female vocalist. Back in the West Vancouver office I'm ecstatic when my tax cheque arrives on a Thursday, but my ecstasy immediately turns to fear when I see the same suits walk past the office window on a Friday. I recognise the same Dept of Immigration officers and my mind is racing ... "can I pull off a fake Canadian accent? Can I pretend I'm someone else?" I surrender in despair, as I sense I sealed my own fate in filing for the tax return. Gerd is distraught, attends my court hearing and pleads my case offering me a work sponsorship. The judge is sympathetic but it's all to no avail as I've already broken the law. Working without a proper work visa, I am presented with the same ultimatum Mick faced. I choose to pay my own way home to Australia. That way I will be allowed back into Canada at a future time and I can start the immigration process when I get back to Australia. They never locked me up though, and I had time to say goodbye to Gerd, Richard, Pete and everyone else I knew in Vancouver. I flew out to Australia wearing my rock star costume, carrying my guitar.

Stephen Trigwell

Marry Your Best Friend

That was the end of Stage Two of my life. Stage One had been childhood, growing up at home and through school, through adolescence, all the while pretty much under parental guidance. I was about to enter Stage Three. The thought of detailing the next forty years of my life is incredibly daunting. I can't possibly recall all the twists and turns. Unintentionally, I'll leave out important moments and milestones ... this can only ever be half a story so, forgive me all the memories filed under "Glen". I do know, Glen and I had known each other for a long time before I committed to a real adult relationship. Our parents would say we sowed our wild oats as young singles and left nothing on the table - the difference was, I had more oats to sow. After we married, and in conversation with Glen, I would always say I was a late maturer. It was true, and it worked brilliantly to deflect my shortcomings. She knew all my silly habits, all my foibles, all my weaknesses, my vanity, my shallowness - but somehow, she forgave me all that. I always knew she loved me.

Let's begin this Love Story.

While I was jaunting around the World, Glen was doing the same through Europe and North Africa in a green kombi with seven others. She'd made plans with her best friend Steph Clarke, to live their own backpacker dream, boarding the Kota Singapora out of

Fremantle on June 14th 1976, sailing to Singapore before flying to London. Two travellers quickly became six however, when they met four intruders on the ship. Sandy from Sydney and Sam, Grant and Gerry, all from Victoria, had made similar plans. A few drinks at the bar and it wasn't long before Sam and Sandy were together, Grant teamed up with Steph, and Gerry and Glen became an item. On arrival in London, the group expanded to include Glen's cousin Phill and his wife Judy, before they set off to conquer Europe. I could cut to the chase and reveal Grant ends up marrying Steph, Sandy and Sam live happily ever after back on Sam's Swan Hill farm, and Gerry and Glen split up before I eventually marry Glen. That's all true ... but it would be remiss of me to understate how these relationships, and the journey itself, have helped shape Glen's life. Glen made lifelong friends. Friends that I know are praying so hard, right now for her recovery. On the wall of our garage in Bunbury, Glen has painted their green kombi, the same kombi they shared throughout their tour of Europe, the kombi they were shot at in, it even has the same number plates. Inside the kombi, she has a picture of each person who shared the journey, and I know that every one of them is back on that journey right now.

Upon returning from Canada, I took a job selling stainless steel cookware door to door. I wasn't much good at it to begin with, but gained valuable selling skills and eventually immersed myself in my first business venture - importing handcrafted macramé from Thailand. I took on a partner, a chap I knew named Duncan and we quickly built the business to about 80 employees, selling macramé on party plan similar to the Tupperware sales model. I was renting with my younger brother Gerry and, even though he was putting in long hours studying, he still found time to party. We were frequenting Hannibals, Eagle One, Gobbles and Adrian's, all nightclubs in Perth.

Plastic Bertrand's Ca Plane Pour Moi and Michael Jackson's Don't Stop 'Till You Get Enough were getting dance floor airplay, as was MiSex with Computer Games and The Eagles with The Long Run. Mick was the bartender at Hannibals and it was about this time I started eating red meat again, as the midnight hamburgers next door to Hannibals were as good as the space invaders video table we ate them off. My reversion to carnivore was complete when I started ordering pepperoni on my late-night pizza. If we were still hungry at 2am, we'd pop upstairs to the Il Trovatore, an illegal casino on the corner of James and Lake Streets for free sandwiches to drunk punters. Macramé World did so well in the first year or so I planned a second trip to Canada, only this time I asked my Mum and Dad if they were interested in accompanying me on the trip as I knew Dad had spent his wartime air force training in Winnipeg, Manitoba. They jumped at the idea and together we shared many wonderful memories discovering the eastern provinces, Montreal and Ottawa plus the usual tourist haunts such as Niagara Falls and the revolving restaurant atop CN Tower in Toronto. On reaching Vancouver, I left them to cruise the inland passage to Alaska, while I spent time with Pete, Richard and Gerd. It had been a bureaucratic nightmare with the Canadian Dept of Immigration to gain re-entry, but it was worth it to share such valuable time with my parents. Returning to Australia and Macramé World, I found I was no longer living in South Perth. While I was away, Gerry and Spider had moved my gear to 128 Hale Rd, in Wembley. I was hunting for a new business idea as I knew macramé had a limited lifespan as a product. In my travels through North America and Canada, I'd seen the popularity of hot tubs and figured it had potential in Australia. I started to do some research. I knew absolutely nothing about hot tubs of course, but registered the name Turbo Tubs in Western Australia after seeing the product advertised nationally in Australian Playboy magazine.

Hmmm ... it must have been someone else's copy or, maybe I saw it in a doctor's surgery? Duncan and I flew to Sydney and persuaded the national distributor to give us access to his western red cedar and Californian redwood hot tub kits, since we controlled the rights to the business name in Western Australia. He agreed. How could he refuse when I was wearing my rock star costume? We bought a delivery van and I basically did a crash course in procurement, logistics, marketing, tradesman contracting, installation and marketing. After a few sales, I wrote a "do it yourself" instruction manual for kit assembly and we started advertising. I sold and installed a tub in City Beach to the owner of the Il Trovatore illegal casino. I finally got some blackjack money back.

It was about this time I visited Glen's parents in Bunbury and learnt that Glen was in Perth. She was living in Subiaco, working at St John's Hospital studying to become a midwife. I was keen to catch up but this time, for the first time in our relationship, I was ready to give instead of take. I arranged to meet her for lunch at the Parmelia Hotel on the corner of Mill St and St George's Terrace. It was so good to see her again and, as I reached my hand across the table, we both knew our relationship had changed forever. I escorted Glen to her graduation as a midwife, and finally found the courage to ask her to marry me. By today's lofty standards, it wasn't a memorable proposal. I'm embarrassed to admit I was lying in bed, leaned across and said "how about we get married?" Glen said yes and started planning immediately. She did everything, I did nothing, the perfect team. It was a good time, I was twenty-seven years old, she was twenty-six and, after eleven years and numerous continents, we were both ready to marry our best friend. By this stage, her father Johan, or Joop as he was known, was in hospital with early stage throat cancer and Glen asked if we could visit him in St John of God

Hospital Bunbury. I asked him for his daughter's hand in marriage while he was lying in bed and, as the tears welled in his eyes, I knew Glen had timed the visit perfectly. I promised him I would love and look after his little princess forever, and that's what I'm doing.

Turbo Tubs was off to a good start ... little did we realise on 29th July 1981, as we lay together on Glen's couch and marvelled at the pomp and majesty of Charles and Diana's wedding, that within months we would both be living in Donnybrook and Bunbury, living totally different lives. We'd sold and installed quite a few tubs, were having fun and excitedly making plans, however over the months business slowed to a trickle, and we were just ticking over, gradually running out of cash. The macramé product life cycle was coming to an end and we were unprepared and under resourced for the advertising onslaught the fibreglass pool incumbents would bring against wooden hot tubs. In hindsight, we probably should have looked into importing home furnishings and other giftware from Asia, as that market was just emerging. Shoulda, woulda, coulda ... I don't do it. Turbo Tubs failed and I was shattered. I hadn't yet learnt that failure was part of success, that the two were in fact the same, both illusions. Like hot and cold water, different manifestations of the same thing.

Glen was my rock. She never doubted me. She picked me up at my lowest and filled me with hope. We decided to move south, Glen to her folks in Bunbury and me to mine in Donnybrook. We regrouped. Our wedding was planned for August 14th 1982.

My Dad asked me if I would take a drive with him, down south and into the wheatbelt. I agreed. I'm sure Mum put him up to it. It was a funny few days, Dad wanted to comfort me, to talk to me and get close, but there were long periods of silence. Not awkward silence, just silence. Dad offered me the chance to work on the farm and in the tearooms while I sorted myself out. Thinking about it now, it was a bit Mike & the Mechanics "The Living Years" ... we were just different generations I guess. I loved my Dad dearly, and still do, but he was the policeman from the military background and I was the hippie son ... the archetypal product of the social revolution. I began working on the family farm, and in Mum and Dad's Donnybrook tearooms again. I was good at it, and I know Mum was grateful for some help with the long hours. Glen began a 23-year career as a midwife at St John of God Hospital in Bunbury. She would make many lifelong friends who are right now praying for her recovery.

Glen and I had a great respect for each other's private, secret memories. What happens in Vegas stays in Vegas. I never wanted or needed to know the details of Glen and Gerry's relationship. As singles we had always led separate lives, she knew of my other dating and my affair with Marilyn but she never asked about it ... it was all history. Glen and Gerry were very close for a long time and after travelling, Glen moved to Swan Hill and nursed at the hospital there for a while, all the while dating Gerry. He owned a wheat and sheep farm, but Glen owned the fantastic story about two orphan lambs she nursed, Minnie and Molly. After bottle rearing them they followed her everywhere, travelling in her car to the shops and, basically wherever Glen went, the lambs were sure to go. It broke her heart when she left Swan Hill to return home to Western Australia and had to leave the lambs with the flock. Gerry promised her he would never sell the lambs. Many years later on a holiday to Swan Hill, Glen stood by a fenced paddock and called to an enormous flock of sheep. Only two sheep looked up - Minnie and Molly. They came bolting over and Minnie immediately lay down on the ground, for Glen to rest her head, just as they had done years before.

It rained, but the sun shone on St Patrick's Cathedral, Bunbury on August 14th 1982. We never got wet. At the reception, I made a nervous speech before Glen's grandmother Mrs. Patterson (Mrs. P) smashed out a few tunes on the upright piano in the ballroom of the Rose Hotel. In her younger days, Mrs. P was a renowned pianist for silent movie cinemas, she was chuffed at being asked to play.

Our wedding was a great day and from that day forward I began my apprenticeship as a married man. Right up until my last day as a bachelor I had been a naughty boy - drunk at 2am standing outside Glen's parent's house yelling for Glen to wake up and telling her how much I loved her. Her father was not impressed, but forgave me, maybe it was the Dutch submariner in him having pity on a young man who should have known better.

I suddenly feel an urgency as I'm tapping out this story. It occurs to me that I want Glen to wake up before the story and my recollections catch up to the present. It feels like an imperative, as two diaries converge towards a collision. As I gently rub her feet and talk to her, I'm aware my story is no longer about ICP, BP, fentanyl and Propofol. This story will change, just as my life did the day I married. Dylan arrives and nurse Tahn explains Glen is about to go for a CT scan and the tracheotomy is planned for after lunch. Dyl asks Glen to wiggle her toes if she understands about the tracheotomy, she does. We assure her she is safe and in good care. I send this text to Hannah and Jake: "Just spoke with Doc Steve ... they want to see results of scan first before disciplinary meeting and tracheotomy. They just kicked us out for tests and scheduled scan. There goes Glen now. Doc Steve just said trach may actually be done tomorrow ... no absolute urgency for this arvo. I told him

I can sign the consent today. Dyl going skateboarding, I'm going to Claremont Quarter then maybe a sleep before returning later this arvo". I drive straight to Mick's. I'm stuffed as I didn't stop writing until 3am. Waking at 2.48pm I see a text from Dylan: "I was just calling regarding the consent form. The ICU Doctor was looking for you. I said I'd call and gain permission to sign it on your behalf. We went into the meeting area and talked about the scan and I tried to call you, I mentioned to him that you probably wouldn't pick up because you were asleep. He said no problem and he would catch up with you tomorrow morning sometime between 0815-0900 most probably. The scan results indicate no new bleeds which was good and that there is still swelling but it has improved since the last scan. So, all in all a pretty good scan. I'm in waiting area as they are rolling Mum before I go in." Dylan lets me in, I'm by Glen's bedside at 3.10pm. Tahn gets me a cup of tea and egg sandwich. It's nice to be back and Dylan is excited when Glen moves her right leg and arm at the same time while Tahn is asking about his unborn baby scans. Glen's brother Charlie and his wife Shirl arrive at 3.50pm. Dyl and I swap out to the waiting room. I'm excited but a little dubious when they report that Glen moved her LEFT foot on command. When I re-enter ICU at 5.20pm Tahn confirms this huge step forward before I get a chance to ask her about it. This is really great news, but until I see it myself, I'm not going to proclaim in a general text to the army.

Our first years of married life are a blur. My parents had bought the other side of their duplex home, atop the hill overlooking Donnybrook townsite, and the small two-bedroom brick and tile dwelling would become our home until 1989. We delayed starting a family for two years even though we both desperately wanted children. We were living week to week, living entirely on Glen's nursing wages as "the farm" could not afford to pay me. I registered for unemployment benefits, and took a short-term job pruning fruit trees for a local Italian family in between working on the farm. Donnybrook has a long and rich Italian migrant history, and having made such a massive contribution to the area, they have earned the respect of everyone. I was still working in the tearooms in Donnybrook, pulling a small wage to alleviate any pressure on the farm budget - but it was Glen who would keep us from drowning financially. As time passed, "the farm" was able to advance me a fuel allowance, followed later by a weekly stipend of $50. A local lead guitar legend Johnny Wenc, dropped into the tearooms while I was practicing one day, and asked if I was interested in starting a band. It was 1981, I was 28 years of age and had never been in a band so jumped at the opportunity to play alongside my childhood hero. We took a drive to Kosmic Music in Victoria Park, where Johnny recommended I buy a Fender twin reverb amp and Shure SM58 microphone. I bought an ex hire amp, which they told us was used on the Roy Orbison 1972 Australian tour. Johnny pulled together some experienced musos, Jimmy on drums and Greg on bass. As the rookie draft pick, I was lead vocalist on rhythm guitar, while Johnny played lead. We rehearsed twice a week in the cold concrete shower block of the "Cardinals Football Club" in Boyanup, sixteen kilometres from Donnybrook, putting together an initial repertoire of about 50 songs. I gave up smoking marijuana right there, forever, as I felt it was affecting my memory for lyrics. By the time we took our first gig at the Bunbury Golf Club, we were pumped to entertain. We started with some slower songs, The Eagles Tequila Sunrise, followed by Max Merritt and the Meteors Slippin' Away. They were dancing by the third song, and by the end of the second bracket it was the Angels, Mental as Anything, Dire Straits and Aussie Crawl. The Propellers were off and running. I burnt out two Sony Walkman's and cut countless headphone leads with the power secateurs as I pruned fruit trees, all the while learning lyrics and new songs. The Propellers took off and we were getting regular gigs in Dunsborough, Bunbury and Collie hotels. We added a keyboard player from Margaret River, and began including INXS and Steely Dan songs while rehearsing in Margaret River. Steve Robinson from Settlers Tavern in Margaret River had us on a four-week rotation as did Peter David at Superflys nightclub in Bunbury. The visiting US navy sailors were loving Jack n Dianne by John Mellencamp and Nightmoves by Bob Seger. We added Luke de Bona to our line up and with Luke on sax, our repertoire expanded to include new songs like Who Can It Be Now by Men at Work and some big songs like Baker Street by Gerry Rafferty. Peter David at Superflys offered us a Bunbury residency, meaning we would play every night, rehearse whenever we want, leave our gear set up and make extra money. We all had other commitments so we turned it down. Russell and I were growing cash crops like potatoes, peas and garlic while planting tangelo, peach, apricot, nectarine, apple, pear and plum trees. Russ's wife Fran was an invaluable worker, picking, sorting and packing produce. At lunch times, after hand picking potatoes for five hours in the summer heat, I would lie on the floor in exhaustion for thirty minutes before going back out and doing it all again for another four or five hours. After work, I would come home covered in brown dirt, sometimes mud, squeeze in a quick shower and spend some time with Glen, before she sped off in our little black Mazda dressed in her white uniform. On a Friday before gigs, I would try to catch a couple of hours sleep before hopping into my old kombi, piled high with all the PA gear and my personal music stuff. I had a little checklist written, right down to the various costumes I sometimes wore. Once, I shaved half of my moustache off, nobody in the crowd even noticed so I grew half a beard - finally they noticed.

Stephen Trigwell

The Dream

Alongside Fran, Glen helped plant some of the fruit trees as we expanded the orchard. Not because she knew how - she just wanted to help. We were all working hard, but not really pushing ahead financially so, we decided to expand the orchard from ~12 acres to what would ultimately become 55 acres. To fund this expansion, we were growing 60,000 cauliflowers every winter and pumpkins in summer, as well as harvesting our own burgeoning fruit crops. During apple harvest, our Dad, Murray, would drive our small red International tractor, delivering and positioning empty bins, as well as removing the full bins back to the shed. With us picking on elevating work platforms known as "squirrels", Dad the great white shark, as we called him, would often surround us with so many bins we couldn't move. At conclusion of our own harvest, we'd also pick apples "off farm" for other growers, Russell and I would each pick 4 rectangular bins per day, a bin holding 24 bushels or 600 kilograms. The rectangular bins were eventually superseded by smaller square bins holding 400 kilos as cool storage stacking became widespread. We never pocketed the extra money, it always went into consolidated farm revenue.

We had an older International tractor, with a set of forks on the front and with the driver's seat hanging, seemingly suspended in mid-air, off the back. There was no cab, no roll bars and it had a diesel motor. We always parked it on a hill because it was notoriously difficult to start. To start the engine, I would hop aboard and half turn the key to heat the glow plug, then, while holding the steering wheel with my left hand, lean forward into a semi standing position before releasing the foot brakes to begin rolling downhill. As the beast bounced and lurched gathering speed, using my right hand, I would reach forward and spray Aerostart down the air intake while simultaneously dropping the clutch. The old "Praying Mantis" as we called it, would roar to life and take off at speed. The trick was to drop the clutch at the right time, before losing control and smashing into the shed. It was a dangerous operation but, at the time it had to be done, so we did it. By now I was pulling $500 per month plus fuel from the farm and Glen was working night shift. $100 per gig came in handy but through all these years Glen was always, by far, our main family breadwinner.

No matter how hard we both worked, we just couldn't seem to get ahead, and Glen was becoming increasingly despondent at not having the opportunity to start a family. She was nearly 31 years old, and our parental window was slipping away. We decided to bite the bullet and just believe that everything would turn out ok. We started trying for children. Almost immediately, Glen fell pregnant and we were ecstatic. About this time, Russell and I started drawing $1000 a month each from the farm and the band was gigging regularly. We had a new drummer in Lance, new songs from U2, Midnight Oil, The Cars and XTC ... and a new name, Serious Jelly. Our repertoire included one of the first songs I ever wrote, called High Times on the Boulevard, a catchy chorus but an eminently forgettable song overall. Glen worked right through her pregnancy until just before Christmas 1984. In preparation for the arrival of our first child, we sold our sporty black Mazda and bought a brand-new Ford Falcon sedan, in those days Donnybrook had its own Ford dealer. Hannah Jayne Trigwell was born at 7.08am on January 14th 1985, at St. John of God Hospital, Bunbury. Glen was dutifully spoilt by all her midwifery workmates, and Sister Killian made sure she had the best of love and care while in hospital. I was still putting in long hours on the farm, but with Hannah snug in the backseat capsule, we would take regular weekend drives to Balingup, Nannup, Ferguson Valley and the nearby countryside. Most Sundays we would drive to Bunbury, where Glen's Mum Nel would always cook up a lunch feast of Indonesian style dishes. While Glen relaxed with her Mum and often grabbed a snooze, Joop and I would go fishing at the Spur, a rocky breakwater on the Indian Ocean. With my parents living next door to us in Donnybrook, we felt we had plenty of support. We built a pergola on the western side of the house as the summer sun made Hannah's bedroom so hot it was uncomfortable. After collecting flat rocks from the hillside, we laid a pathway to wind its way amongst the plants. I was strangely satisfied when told the rocks were probably stacked by early settler convicts, possibly under the supervision of my great, great grandfather, Sergeant Henry Trigwell - the first Trigwell to set foot in Australia arriving Fremantle in 1851.

I leave ICU and Tahn at 5.56pm. Tracey has cooked a lovely meal of chicken schnitzel and vegetables and I'm in bed by 10pm after sending this text: "No tracheotomy today ... now scheduled for ~9-10am tomorrow. Good scan today, no more bleeding ... quiet day response wise but doctors still confident in time. Not expecting too much response tomorrow either ... day after could be very interesting though. Thank you all"

Tues 1st June

I'm in ICU at 8.10am. Hannah, Dylan and I are called into a meeting with Doctor Steve to sign the consent form for the tracheotomy. I hate this little meeting room. Every time we go in there we get either bad news or come out feeling flat. He doesn't let me down and today is no different. Dr Steve is a very nice guy, but the words "SEVERE right-side brain infarction" are ringing in all our ears. He talks of possible full left side body deficit - no left arm, no left leg, permanent wheelchair, for the first time we hear of possible feeding issues. There is a possibility she will need to be fed permanently by gastric tube. Dr Steve says he cannot guarantee Glen will regain swallow and gag reflex. We all look at each other. I thought we were winning? This is supposed to be getting better? Dr Steve says some families decide not to go ahead with a tracheotomy as they are under instructions from the patient not to go down that path. This is a frightening conversation and all I can think of is my last discussion with Prof Lind. Hannah has tears in her eyes ... I don't look at Dylan. I mention my conversation with Prof Lind and his prognosis of the likelihood of full right arm, full right leg, full vision, full speech, probability of rehab on left leg and possibility of reversal of tracheotomy. Dr Steve agrees all that is possible.

The unknown is, how much of that scenario will manifest when Glen awakens. Maybe, because Dr Steve himself was going to perform the tracheotomy, just maybe, he was accentuating the risks? We ask have they changed their timeline for Glen to awaken? He says she is already semi awake, responding to commands, just not fully functional. All things are possible, simultaneously. I sign the form, we *leave the room. Again, we sit in silence. Another Molotov cocktail. Devastation mixed with hope. I'm shaken but not stirred. This girl will awaken, and she will astound these guys. June 6th is coming into focus, it's only 5 days away. It's been a date of significance for me since leaving for Africa on June 6th, 1974. Our granddaughter Addi was born June 6th and I dropped my first single Autumn Day, on all major streaming platforms June 6th. Maybe June 6th will be the day Glen comes back to us? I put it in my calendar - June 6th Glen wakes up at 10.30am. They come to prepare for the tracheotomy, we leave. Hannah drives me back to her place where Kade has taken the day off. Dylan goes solo skateboarding in Kings Park. What started as a day to kick goals has shifted to one of worrisome defence. At 12.08pm I get a call from the unknown number. Glen is ok and the tracheotomy is a success. Hannah and I head straight to ICU and Glen is looking better without the ventilator in. Dr Steve comes around at 3.50pm and asks Glen to respond to certain commands ... she moves her right arm, right fingers and right leg and toes, as well as her left foot. He then asks her to bend her left leg at the knee and she made a deliberate slight bend there - only slight, but I'm really encouraged by that as that is the first time I have seen her move her left knee at all. This is brilliant. As we've come to expect, Glen did not move her left arm or fingers. I hate giving up on anything - but is it a lost cause? Prove me wrong darling. Dylan and Jake take over, so I pop back to McNeil St where Mick and Tracey's daughter, Sophie, has prepared a delicious meal of sautéed Tasmanian salmon with charred brussel sprouts, broccoli, peas and mini carrots. Afterwards, I shoot back to ICU and sit with Glen until 9.00pm. Just before sleeping, I meditate for about thirty minutes.*

Wed 2nd June

8.00am. As I reach the green lifts my brother Gerry calls me from Coral Bay, 1100 kilometres north of Perth. We chat about Glen, me, our kids and life in general. At 10am they ask me to leave while they move Glen from the bed to a chair. Dylan arrives at 11am and I'm feeling nervous because Glen is not really responding to our commands as she was yesterday. The nurse does some pain tests, and Glen immediately responds and starts moving to command. Maybe she was sleeping? Maybe just exhausted from the move? Glen squeezes Dylan's hand on his request and I shed a tear. She's back.

When Hannah turned six months old I quit the band and Serious Jelly folded. We were playing at least once every weekend, occasionally twice, travelling between Harvey, Margaret River, Bunbury and Collie. With Glen returning to work at St. John's and the farm becoming more and more intensive, something had to give. I could have given music away for good right then, but Glen wouldn't hear of it. She encouraged me to partition a small section inside our garage and it became my new practice room. A seventeen-year-old local boy asked if I would teach him how to play guitar. Mal came every Tuesday night. Besides bad habits, I taught him a few chords, some really basic scales, the rudiments of timing, some vocal coaching and most importantly I think, the love of music. Cheap Trick's "The Flame" was a vocal challenge for sure, but we were happy to try anything.

We undertook a rapid expansion on the farm, pushing out old trees and planting new orchards of Pink Lady and Fuji apples as well as pears, plums, peaches and nectarines. Still growing cauliflowers in winter and pumpkin in summer, we began leasing acreage about 10 kilometres away to grow potatoes. We were so busy our lives simply revolved around the seasons. We were always under the pump to finish pruning by end of winter, under pressure to walk every row of cauliflower at harvest, having to control fungal disease in crops after rain, harvest fruit within a given harvest window. The days became weeks and the months became years. I used to love being surprised around breakfast time, when Gerd would occasionally call from Canada and remind me of my past life. Glen would recognise his loud accent and, listening to their flirty banter always brought a smile to my face. Gerd was always a cheeky guy but Glen was more than a match for his repartee.

Farmers by nature are all optimists, they have to be. When you plant a seed, you have to believe it will grow and grow well. When you plant a tree, you must be able to visualise it in years to come with a full crop. When the dams are empty and dry, you must innately believe the rains will come. Every year was a re-evaluation and a reset of the dream. We would each take two weeks annual leave, Russ in early summer before harvest, and me in winter immediately post-harvest. While Russ was away I'd keep an eye on irrigation schedules and crop load management, a manual process known as thinning ... where small fruitlets are taken from the tree to limit the crop load, thereby guaranteeing larger fruit at harvest. We employed teams of backpackers, as it was a massive task over many weeks. My job was to record which rows had been done, who did it, how many trees they did and how long it took. At the height of the season we sometimes had 30 backpackers on the payroll. Our two-week holiday block could only ever be taken in winter, so Glen would purposefully save for a family holiday somewhere warm. Over the years we visited Bali a few times, Thailand, Queensland, Sarawak, Exmouth, Broome and Monkey Mia. My good mate Johnny Luscombe would call every year and ask if I could accompany him on a fishing trip to the Abrolhos Islands, an archipelago off Geraldton. For years I had to say no, because I couldn't afford time away from the farm. Johnny, a very capable and experienced boatie owned a 57-foot Salthouse cruiser. He knew the islands well. I could never accept his offer as it was always during apple picking season and with only 2 weeks a year, it just wasn't possible. I did get there eventually. As our farm workload increased and inflation kicked in, Russell and I went from $1000 to $1500 a month each in drawings. As a one third partner and shareholder in the land, Gerry had never drawn a cent as he was living and working in Perth as an accountant and the farm could not afford to pay a dividend. Every month he would process Russ's raw data into farm accounts then annually, he'd compile and lodge the farm tax return. Our plan of course, was to build the business so it could pay dividends to all shareholders. By the time the last episode of Countdown went to air in July 1987, our turnover was growing steadily but not spectacularly. We were exporting 80% of our produce to Singapore, Hong Kong, United Kingdom and the Middle East but price per kilo for cauliflower was actually coming down.

Thurs 3rd June

Jake has postponed flying back to Roy Hill (where he works) until Monday 7th. Glen went for another CT scan at 10am and upon our return into ICU, I notice her left eye is open. I send this text to Hannah and Dylan: "Jake is with me in ICU waiting room, just kicked out for trachie tests. When Glen came back from scan her left eye was open. I asked Glen to squeeze my fingers with her right hand if she could see me and she did. Awesome. It didn't stay open for long but she looked tired from the scan I think. The nurse told me she opened the eye on the way to the scan so that is good. Big step forward". At last a good step forward ... I feel better. It's hard to differentiate between underlying long-term brain damage and temporary swelling disability. All the doctors are telling us only time will tell now.

Hannah was nearly 2 years old when we decided to try for another baby. We were still living in the two-bedroom duplex on the hill overlooking Donnybrook, when Dylan James Trigwell came into our world on 23rd October 1986 at 2 minutes past midnight. He was a perfect little boy in every way but how can I paint only half a picture? While I was busy on the farm, Glen was becoming the matriarch of our young family and growing into an amazing and wonderful mother. As the weeks passed, I looked forward to Mal's visits and we would often play deep into the night, sometimes just rolling over chord progressions until Mal became a very adept lead guitarist in a short time. I was unaware of it, but our kids must have been listening intently as they lay in bed, because years later Dylan and Hannah would remember the songs we practiced and often cue them on Spotify. After a few months Mal began writing original songs and, of his own accord, became a way better guitarist than I, with a very handy Paul Kelly type voice. He formed his own band, playing many local pubs and backing up Aussie legend Matt Taylor and Chain at a local festival.

Even though Glen and I often felt exhausted, we loved being parents, always laughing and playing with Hannah and Dylan. It was a joy to rediscover all the wonderful things in the world through the eyes of a child. Both sets of grandparents were a gift, appreciated and loved by the toddlers and us. In the spring of 1988, we all flew to Broome where Karen, a midwifery colleague and ex housemate of Glen, picked us up and drove to Bidyadanga about 200 kilometres south of the town. We were privileged to stay a week at the Aboriginal Community, enjoying the hospitality, amazing fishing and sharing beautiful moments with some of the older women there. It was Kimberley hot, Glen was 8 months pregnant with Jake and she wanted to go for a swim. Karen dropped us off at the sandhills, pointed towards the Indian Ocean and said watch out for the tide it comes in pretty fast. "By the way" she said, "keep your eye out for the skeleton". Sure enough, we came across a real live, or should I say dead, skeleton of a human. Often completely covered in sand, it was regularly exposed by the wind. Well known to the local indigenous people, they reckoned it was not one of theirs and the whites had no record of it either, so I guess we'll just call him Sandy. We patched together a small sun shelter for Glen, using driftwood and beach towels, before I took Hannah and Dylan by the hand and slowly walked out, across the wet sand, exploring the rock pools to the water on the horizon. The tide was out, but the noise from the incoming tide was ominous as it cascaded, rushing towards us. We had no time to lose when I realised, on turning, Glen was now a distant speck in the sandhills. Almost 2 years old and already exhausted from the long walk out, Dylan was spent, I carried him the whole way back while Hannah ran alongside. The tide was relentless and every time we slowed the little wavelets would wash at our feet. By the time we reached the beach I was absolutely stuffed, relieved, and in need of a beer. I gained a real respect for Kimberley tides that day.

We took a drive north, along a coastal bush track to the tidal inlet of Engindine. As we descended the sandstone ridge, I could barely contain my excitement as a magazine fishing opportunity unfolded before my eyes. Karen had to pull me aside and remind me that, as a stranger, and as was custom, it was important I show respect, by first introducing myself to the spirits of the land and the sea. Our guide, a Karajarri grandmother, watched intently as I followed her instructions, taking seawater in my mouth before spitting it back into the moving tide. Later, she cooked an amazing damper bread in the open campfire, to go with the fresh fish thrown straight into the ashes. When cooked, the shrivelled fish guts, skin and scales simply fell away to reveal beautifully cooked soft flesh. Later that evening back at the community, a young indigenous boy gingerly approached me as I played alone, outside on the lawn. He was carrying a guitar almost as big as himself. We played Cherry Bomb by John Cougar Mellencamp. Music, as always was the unspoken language. Our kids and Glen ended up with a bad case of nits in their hair from Bidyadanga, but it was worth it for an unforgettable holiday and an insight into indigenous respect for the land and their culture.

Back on the farm, each season would bring special moments into vivid life and beauty. Dewdrops shone like diamonds, when the first rays of summer sun lit the spider webs, hanging heavy on rusted fence wires. Steam rose from freshly tilled chocolate soil as the earth breathed in, then smoked from our freezing lips as we breathed out. In springtime, silence became a gradual roar as invisible bees buzzed on an overhead flight path between a distant blossom and the hive. In winter, I'd blindly stumble through a pre-dawn mediaeval fog, only to surprise an equally blind cow, we'd just look at each other ... there was nowhere to go. As the sun set on the red persimmon and yellow peach trees, the autumn colours are a gift from God, so beautiful that even a grown man bends and collects the fallen leaves.

Surrounded by all this beauty, the daily mundane tasks turned into the fruitful years. We built a huge shed and cool stores complex, purchased hundreds of wooden harvest bins, new tractors, a forklift, trailers, hydraulic picking platforms, established more trellised orchard and more reticulation. We grew the orchard from a legacy

10-acre block to 55 acres. At one stage we had the largest planting of nashi fruit in Western Australia. We were employing more staff, but continual reinvestment and debt financed expansion meant we never paid a shareholder dividend. The nature of farming is such that there are always new capital expenses, it's like having a tiger by the tail, and we were on a mission. Russell and I went on an orchard improvement group tour to South Africa to study growing techniques and technology innovations.

I like a famous John Lennon quote "Life is what happens to you when you are busy planning other things". How true that is. While Russ and I were busy on the farm, Glen was still nursing Sunday and Monday nights as well as frequent extra shifts and working public holidays, as the loading allowance was attractive. Glen was totally exhausted. In hindsight, I don't know how she did it but, in the midst of this mayhem, on the 29th October 1988, our son Jacob Stephen Trigwell was born at 6.30am in St. John's hospital Bunbury. Our family was complete. We had three children under four years of age sleeping in the small, second bedroom of our two-bedroom duplex. My parents decided to sell the duplex half and "the farm" would build us a new house in the town of Donnybrook. Without success, Glen and I drove around the town searching for a location that would inspire us. We explored each street before finally turning into a cul-de-sac and finding the perfect block, albeit without a "for sale" sign. The land owner turned out to be an old family friend of ours, and lived in the adjacent house. A widow, she had withdrawn the block from sale because she wanted to decide who her new neighbours might be. The quarter acre block was in Boulder Street, facing east for the morning sun, with a wonderful stand of native bush at the back, separating us from the local golf course. After etching our names into the wet cement of the garage floor when the slab was laid, I was thirty-six years old, a year older than Glen when we proudly moved into our new house on Christmas Eve 1989. Joop and Nel stayed the night with us, celebrating our first ever Christmas in Boulder Street to the sounds of laughter and joy ... and Elvis Presley singing Blue Christmas. Glen never, ever, celebrated Christmas without Elvis singing Blue Christmas. For the first time in their lives Hannah, Dylan and Jake each had their own bedroom, but would often drag their mattress into another, to sleep by their brother or sister. We went about furnishing the house, designing reticulation and establishing what would become our perfect garden. Finally, with Charlie helping, we built another pergola, this time with a hot tub. In time, we erected a fence across the back of the block between the house and the bush, perfect for keeping a black Labrador puppy enclosed. The kids adored Jet, but not as much as Joop. Jet ended up eloping, became a city dog, moved to Bunbury and should have been a border security sniffer dog, but instead, lived an idyllic life as companion to both Glen's parents.

Fri 4th June

Coffee at la Galette 8am, ICU by 8.30am. Glen stable overnight and no real change in status. I sit with her all morning before driving to Leighton Beach for lunch with Bob, my drummer from Fuzzyiguana days. Two days now with not a lot of big improvement in Glen. We ask to have a meeting with the ICU Doctor on duty and, at 5pm Doctor Vera sits down and tells us Glen has had a big stroke, will likely have major left side deficit, almost certainly no left arm function, high probability of no left leg. We know all that from our meeting with Dr Steve. She goes on and on, by the end of it all we are all feeling a bit despondent. I'm not sure if it's denial or what, but when we gather at Hannah's for dinner, we unanimously agree that hers is essentially just another opinion. As a family we are struggling with the uncertainty. We stick together, and yes, we do hold on to each and every little sign no matter how small. We are not giving up. In my mind, I see a left arm with possibly no function, and a left leg with potential for rehabilitation, we just don't know the final level of deficit yet. Maybe doctors Steve and Vera are right, but we aren't going to concede ... anything, and we know Glen will never give up. There may also be some level of cognitive (abstract) deficit. I suspect there will be a wheelchair, probably a household elevator/lift, maybe a degree of home care? But I also see a good right arm, a good right leg, speech, hearing, eating, holding grandchildren while seated, watching tv and pushing buttons on the remote, wheelchair walks down town for coffee and across the road to the watch sunsets at the beach. I promised Joop I would look after his princess and I will, I cannot bear to think of any other option.

Riley and Maureen Horrocks moved to Donnybrook in the late 1980's and we immediately struck up a close friendship. Riley was principal at St Mary's Primary School where all our kids attended, and Maureen became the music teacher there. Riley talked me into becoming school treasurer in exchange for a stack of second-hand bricks ... I can't believe I was so cheap! Then, he talked me into playing a season of basketball at age 38. Our families were close by the time he talked me into taking on the role of "statistics man", and half-time motivator for the football team he was coaching. So, when Riley suggested we train for the Bunbury marathon, I said why not? We began by running around the local oval then, for 6 months, we trained every day after work, generally a 10-kilometre run through the town and nearby native bush. Weekends, I would sometimes run a half marathon. Finally, a twelve-kilometre steep run down, and up through a Collie coal mine proved a good lead up preparation run as the marathon event loomed. I was personally running 94 kilometres a week, timing myself, recording my progress and pushing myself hard, chasing PB's. Our final training run was a 28.9-kilometre Sunday run from Donnybrook to Mumballup. As the marathon approached, we tapered our running preparation and carbo loaded in the lead up to the start date. By 3rd May 1992 we were both primed and ready. The run north along Ocean Drive was straight into a brisk north-west wind, with the rain in my face, Glen and the kids travelled slowly alongside, urging me on from our Toyota Tarago. Riley completed the run in 3.20.13 and I finished the run in 3.40.59. I was disappointed with my time, but knew I had lost focus at the 32-kilometre mark when I was very nearly run over by a speeding car. From couch potato to running a marathon within six months eventually became a source of pride and, I felt, a testament to my Space, Time, Energy and Matter theory (STEM). More on STEM later.

Farm production was increasing nicely, Russell and I were drawing more salary, our families were growing and we all had great social lives. Coming home tired after a long day's work, Glen would order me into the kids' room to spend some time with them before they fell asleep. Sometimes I'd read a book, but often I would make up fantasy stories about my day working on the farm. The kids were at an age where they believed everything that came out of their Dad's mouth, and they loved my impossible stories so much it wasn't long before my secret character, Smarty Pants the Fox worked his way into every story. The Horrocks kids loved a sleepover to hear a Smarty Pants story too, and together, they all desperately wanted to disbelieve all of Smarty's ridiculous antics. I spied an actual dead fox on the farm one day and wove the carcass into a story, of course the kids thought this tale was so obviously outlandish they demanded to see the body. I drove them to the evidence. They were dumbstruck and awestruck ... it was true! I'd successfully planted enough doubt for a few more weeks of stories. Smarty was a mischievous, clever and adventurous character always finding himself in deep trouble but of course, always escaping unscathed. Many years later, rifling through old 4 track tapes, I found an audio recording of story time with Smarty. Listening back, I thought it would be an exciting idea to take the children's stories a bit further. The Great Journey: Amazing Adventures with Smarty Pants the Fox was published in 2004, in a small, but successful commercial project linked to a charity foundation. At book launch, we tied a copy of the book to a bunch of helium filled balloons, literally launching Smarty into space from the top of the 15-metre-high poppet head frame over Hunters Venture gold mine. The first signed copy sold for $300 at a charity auction and, together with Kethrine Spence my illustrator, we sold about 2000 copies. Changing life priorities meant the other 4 or 5 stories which made it to manuscript form never got published. On the front cover of The Great Journey, I tongue in cheek wrote "from the yet to be made movie in Donnybrook". Time is a wonderful thing ... you never know.

No Escaping Change

Unfortunately, the farm was never financially strong enough to pay a shareholder dividend. Gerry could see the writing on the wall and wanted out. It became a trying time for all our family as it was the historical family farm owned by three brothers but, we weren't generating enough income to support three families. Gerry had always lived in Perth and was now building his own business in Mandurah, moving back to Donnybrook with the consequent farm income dilution wasn't an option for his family. It became inevitable that Russell and I would buy Gerry's one third share of the farm.

When the original patriarch Henry Trigwell first arrived at Fremantle in 1851, he supervised convicts before resigning to build the Anchor and Hope Inn in Donnybrook, opening 1865. It was a staging inn for passing travellers and horse drawn carriages on their way to and from Bunbury and Perth. For the princely sum of £11 he was granted 30,000 acres from the newly formed Western Australia State Government. It was a fantastic scheme by the Government and very successful in developing the whole of Australia. Others of course, see the scheme as the genesis of a fantastic crime because 150 years later, we are still living with the consequences of bitterness amongst indigenous Australians. Was there a better way of doing it? I don't know. That's just how global expansion unfolded at that point in time. Through the lens of history though, the way it played out has a lot of bad karma to me. I can't complain, as I was ultimately a beneficiary by simply being born white.

Thinking back to my childhood days in Brunswick Junction, I'd catch the rickety old school bus to and from Harvey, a 22-kilometre journey. Every morning there were about 10 young indigenous kids already on the bus, from the Church of Christ mission in Roelands. It was only later in life I realised these kids were children of the stolen generation. My Dad, as the local policeman, was often called to a makeshift bush camp on the banks of the Collie River. It was here, opposite the mission and as close as possible to their children, the parents would drown their sorrow in sadness and despair. The respected elder at the camp would often ring Dad from the Roelands Post Office, and Dad and he would work together to break up domestic violence and alcohol fuelled fights. I challenge any parent to consider what they would do if the Government came unannounced and snatched your children away. I would be absolutely horrified and heartbroken, and couldn't think of anything worse. If my children were literally kidnapped and then I was denied visiting rights, it's quite plausible I could become an alcoholic or lose my mind. It happened. My empathy on this may cause chagrin amongst a few people I know but, I've never had issue with taxpayers compensating indigenous groups and, in my opinion, indigenous Australians have every reason to feel hard done by over the decades. Having said all that - it is what it is. No good can be gained by dwelling on negatives from one's past. I urge everyone to follow this link:

https://catsinam.org.au/2021/03/sadie-canning/

Read the story of Sadie Canning. She was the first triple certificate indigenous nurse in Western Australia and second in the entire nation. Why am I even talking about this? ... because Sadie delivered Glen, in Leonora, in 1954. Native title agreements and compensation are still continually being negotiated, and indigenous culture is rightly recognised in many aspects of modern Australian society, but I don't believe it has to be complicated. For me, the whole idea behind reconciliation is not that difficult: Aussies of European descent, Wadjellas, need to understand and acknowledge ALL of our history, even the bits we should be ashamed of. We need to respect indigenous culture and be proud of our indigenous nation and their heritage. To our indigenous brothers and sisters, you must never forget, and I know it must be so hard to forgive past mistakes, but I urge you to take Sadie Canning's advice word for word ... "don't dwell on the past, it is up to us to succeed or not". No-one, regardless of skin colour, can carry bitterness with them throughout their life and, everyone deserves respect. Lastly, we must all be truly thankful we are able to live in this wonderful country. It is what it is and, we can't change history, but hopefully we can be open minded enough to learn from it. It might be a simple recipe for reconciliation, but I believe it's that simple.

For Henry Trigwell, the conditions of land grant were such that the settler had to fence the property and work it as a productive farm. If the conditions weren't met, the Government would repeal the grant and sell it to another keen settler. The reality of course, was that Henry's 30,000 acres was all rugged bush country, and I'm sure parts of the original grant land must have been rescinded. A zoomed out look at our family history shows earlier generations split their landholding amongst beneficiaries as each generation passed. That works ok until the holding becomes too small or uneconomic. My own father and his two brothers hardly spoke a word to each other in forty years because of a succession plan gone wrong. The three of them worked off farm in separate, unrelated careers. The extended Trigwell family is littered with family feuds and breakups. Not every son or daughter wanted to live and work the same land. Payouts were made, deals were done and estates were divided. Our generation was no different and, although at times it was a highly charged atmosphere, the end result was the same. Russell and I bought Gerry out in about 1995.

Fran and Glen bought a mobile carpet cleaning business around this time and ran it as a partnership for a few years. They did very well through word of mouth, repeat business and a few bigger commercial contracts, working the jobs into their already busy schedules. Glen has a favourite story of the plastic "dog poo" she placed behind a sofa, for Fran to find in total disgust. The cash came in handy and they eventually sold the business for a small capital profit. We were living in our new house in Boulder Street and Mal was still coming around most Tuesday's, for a jam and a bottle or two of McWilliams Tall Ships port. By this stage we had graduated from garage to lounge room. He asked if I wanted to join him in a new band. I felt flattered but was reticent as I thought I was too old. Mal was keen, so we started jamming with Bob Dilollo on drums and Mark Severn, better known as Swervy, on bass. All three were accomplished musicians, and I began to look forward to our practices in Bob's shed on his remote hilltop farm. Our philosophy was simple - have a good time ... and we did. Fuzzyiguana became an alternative rock, country, psychedelic funk band playing covers and originals in Margaret River, Dunsborough, Bunbury, Harvey, Collie, Donnybrook, Bridgetown, Nannup and Greenbushes. As well as a few private shows in Perth, numerous festivals and benefit gigs, we did a memorable show at a tiny country hall in Brookhampton. On that occasion, many of the punters were dressed in costume and my eyes were drawn to a guy with his back to me. He was wearing a black leather jacket with a hand painted peace sign on the back. Sure enough, the Magic Jacket had found a new party. As he turned around I recognised Aaron, a mate of my son Dylan and an ex Old Goldfields employee. The jacket hadn't fitted me for decades and must have been hanging, lost in my wardrobe. Dylan had borrowed it for a fancy-dress party and then loaned it to Aaron. He apologised for besmirching the jacket with a peace sign, but meeting the Magic Jacket again after all those years, at a party of all places, was more than just a peace sign. I told him to keep the jacket. Funny how the world works, maybe one day the Magic Jacket will team up with the electric shaver in Madrid! Fuzzyiguana gained a mini cult following after a succession of energetic stage performances including chain sawing a guitar in half and wearing lizard, police and phantom costumes. As a band we were all living out our rock star fantasies, it was hilarious fun. Strutting on the hotel bar or swinging from the beer garden rafters was de rigueur, but behind the antics, we were all very serious about our sound. We had a strong repertoire of original songs which were favourites with our crowds. The Rudy Zarzoff Tour gave us the opportunity to showcase the band and, at the same time sell a bit of merchandise. At the peak of Fuzzyiguana's popularity we were asked to play alongside Powderfinger and Jebediah at the Donnybrook "Bundy Sundy" Music Festival. Why did we turn it down? It was time. The band had run its course. Swervy moved to Broome, the band broke up shortly after and we never again performed as Fuzzyiguana. We did continue to play, just not in public. Bob's remote farmhouse rehearsal shed became a refuge, where we explored a few different styles and directions without the pressure of having to perform, rediscovering the simple joy of playing together. We were always seeking that moment where the aggregate was more than the sum of the individual parts. That's why muso's play. We knew we'd nailed it one time, when at 2am Bob's wife Sam told us to shut up, after Mal perfected the feedback on David Bowie's Heroes. Probably the best part about playing with Bob, Swervy and Mal is that we have all grown (older?) together. Years later, we did reform and played out regularly as Stickfish, with a plethora of originals from both Mal and myself. We never really got into serious recording though, which in hindsight was a mistake I think. As part time musical collaborators, we've each gone thru big life changes over the years and, I consider myself extremely fortunate to have had the opportunity to play alongside such talented musos.

Glen's brother Charlie calls and asks if he and Shirley can visit Glen at 3pm. As they walk in to ICU waiting room Dylan rocks up ... so it's Dylan, Jake, Charl, Shirl and myself in rotation to see Glen as they only allow two in at a time. We are all in need of a sign of progress, to give us renewed faith that Glen is still slowly improving. Jake sends me this text: "Dad come in if you're still waiting Mum is listening at the moment, a few hand squeezes". Charlie also gets a hand squeeze and he's chuffed. I'm back in ICU at 4.12pm holding Glen's hand and she is squeezing. When I tell her I have to go, she squeezes harder. Later that night I get this text from Jake: "Really good signs from Mum tonight Dad, I know Dyl's been sending them on too but she woke up about 3 or 4 times with eye open and hand squeezing/holding, also whilst she was squeezing my hand one time she rubbed her thumb on my hand for a while which was awesome! Really, really good! Hope she is even more awake tomorrow that would be nice! Have a good night tonight love ya" At last we get some progress with Glen. I refuse to believe the worst-case scenario.

I'm filled with renewed hope and send back a message of encouragement to the kids: "Fark ... you guys are awesome ... that is such good news ... we are winning we are fucking winning!"

Sat 5th June

I'm awake at 5.50am ready to meet Gerry. He's driven down from Coral Bay and I've arranged to meet him for coffee and breakfast at la Galette. We shared a few non-alcoholic beers at the Hamptons in City Beach last night. After brekky he'll take a leisurely 417-kilometre drive to Geraldton, stay the night then continue north back to Coral Bay. He's a good brother, as is my eldest brother Russell. We were raised by loving parents and I know they would be proud we are all friends, no family fireworks.

Stephen Trigwell

Back to the Future

After Russ and I bought Gerry's one third share of the farm, it became imperative we maximise and realise the farm potential, after all, between us we had five children of our own. We were the first generation of Trigwell brothers to actually work together on the same land, over a generation, to build the business. Most farmers are price takers, meaning they are forced to take whatever market prices prevail. Generally, they are not price makers and, if they are, it isn't for very long because other farmers start doing whatever it is they are doing. A new variety of fruit for instance, only attracts a premium until it becomes a widely planted commodity. We knew we had to find a sustainable edge. On our Sunday drives, I regularly noticed car loads of Asian tourists stopping on the roadside to take pictures of the fruit trees. In the mid to late nineties there was nothing in Donnybrook for tourists to do. Nothing. There was no tourist infrastructure. The only attraction in town, the local Deer Park, had closed down. Donnybrook was the town everyone would drive through on their way to somewhere else. Small town renewal expert Peter Kenyon named Donnybrook WA's ugliest town, and one of the ugliest in the nation, "Donnybrook's streetscape was so barren people just wanted to keep on driving" he said. The town did however, have a legitimate and exciting gold mining history but, except for a few old timers, most residents were totally unaware of it. The biggest and most exciting of the mines was right on our farm property. My mind was ticking over ... Asian tourists, no tourism competition, unique gold mining history, pick your own fruit, direct fruit sales, photo ops. etc. Then the questions, how do we make money? What are our products? It's ok to have multitudes of tourists walking around the farm but what are we actually selling them? Boutique wineries were common throughout the South West but no-one was making cider or fresh apple juice. I searched the internet for cider makers anywhere in Australia and could find only one listing ... Kellybrook Winery in Victoria. Glen and I, with the kids flew to Melbourne, and we visited Darren Kelly in the Yarra Valley. He only had one cider - a scrumpy, an old English style of cider in a brown 750 ml bottle with a cork seal. It was high alcohol at 12.5%, essentially a fruit wine and a very poor relation to their range of grape wines. I went back to Donnybrook and started experimenting with cider home brews. We came up with a business plan that we felt would appeal to a wide demographic and varied interest groups: Build a farm tearoom/cafe offering food, art, local handicrafts, jewellery, coffee, corporate function facilities. Build a separate cidery and incorporate a cellar door into the tearooms with a full range of orchard grown ciders and juices. Sell fresh fruit as well as provide a "pick your own" experience. Reconstruct the poppet head over the original mine, then build a museum to house the Donnybrook gold mining history and offer a gold panning experience. Stock the vast farm dam with trout and silver perch, and allow tourists to experience catching their own fish. Construct 8 marron (freshwater crayfish) aquaculture ponds, with aquaculture shed, bio filtration system and 7 grow out tanks for trout, silver perch and marron. Plant beautiful gardens around the tearooms and build an al fresco area with sandpit for toddlers and a live music venue for adults. Push out a few rows of fruit trees to enhance the view across the water and build a children's playground. Conduct farm tours of the orchard, cidery, aquaculture and mining. Build a corporate website with online shop and market the newly branded business. Basically, we wanted to make the venue so interesting, people would stay for longer and eventually, get hungry and thirsty. It was an ambitious transformation of the business.

Sitting by Glen's bedside holding her hand I'm falling asleep, so when we're asked to leave at 1pm, I grab the opportunity for a quick snooze in Peppy Grove. Mick makes a cup of tea and we talk about Glen. I have been texting people updates on Glen, sucking energy, and I know many people are praying for her recovery. As a consequence, I find myself as the unsuspecting General of a veritable army of well-wishers, a literal congregation of people praying. I see every little change on the battlefield and I need to keep them informed and positive, but at the same time, fully aware of the dangers we face. I am reminded of the time I read The Art of War by Sun Tzu, when he breaks all recognised rules of war to camp his army between the enemy and a river. His troops of course know this is a death wish and are bewildered by his orders. Sun Tzu fears they are greatly outnumbered and his choice of location is deliberate, to extract a superhuman effort from his army. They win the battle. I burst into tears as I explain to Tracey that my biggest fear is if Glen doesn't wake up. We are all holding onto little signs but I dread the inevitable conversation if we don't win this. The ICU waiting room is a revolving door of utter tragedy and despair, and I deliberately haven't written about the families I have seen come and go, numb from being smacked in the face by a piece of four by two. I think of the young man with the bloodshot eyes again. His Dad died a day later. I couldn't help but overhear the conversation about organ transplant donation. There are no words for the heartbreak in ICU. I'm trying so hard to remain positive - for myself, for my kids, for all of our friends and relatives and for the army. In my private moments, I know the most effective rehab is in the first three months after a stroke. Glen is nearly 3 weeks in already and hasn't properly woken up yet. I know all the doctors and nurses in ICU by name, and Paula the receptionist gives me special treatment. I feel like the old guy, the OG, the veteran of ICU. I believe firmly in the power of Love, God, whatever you want to call it, and I know we can conquer this goliath, but I am also the General in the corner backed up against the river, praying for a miracle. I'm back at the hospital by 4pm. They've transferred Glen from ICU to High Dependency Unit (HDU) and Jake has been with her since about 11am. Dylan has gone back to Bunbury to be with his wife Karlee and daughter Addison on her 3rd birthday tomorrow, June 6th. If ICU is the ward of despair, then HDU is the ward of hope ... patients sometimes walk out of here. I hope I don't end up the old veteran of HDU.

Dave Pender and his wife Anne came to us and asked if he could run his metal detector over the old Hunters Venture Mine dump on the farm. He was a prospector from Hill End in New South Wales and they were travelling around the goldfields of WA. We consented, and in conversation we learnt he had built a poppet head frame over a mine in NSW. He showed us a picture of the one he built, it was reminiscent of a giant water tank stand. We had an old black and white picture of the original Hunters Venture Gold Mine, taken in 1899. It had a massive two-level poppet head frame 15 metres high, with a winding wheel at the apex and a gantry leading off one side. The gantry itself was a walkway platform which carried a small rail system, with kibbles for dumping overburden onto the mine dump. We asked Dave if he could build an exact replica of the 1899 structure over the old shaft. He studied the old image. Based on two men and a dog in the foreground, he was able to draw to scale a design plan, with an estimated 3 month build timeline including total materials and labour cost. We commissioned Dave immediately and he began building January 4th 1996. While his wife Anne packed fruit in our pack house, Dave built the entire structure using hand tools, a generator and a chainsaw, finishing on April 4th, the day before Good Friday, exactly three months from when he started. At the end of construction, all that remained of the estimated materials was a small pile of wood chips. He had predicted the materials perfectly. He built it as a kit on the ground and, when we crane hoisted it into position it was perfect, he did not have to drill or re-drill any other holes. He was a genius. I invited two old mining identities on the day we re- erected the poppet head over the Hunters Venture shaft. Ron Smith was the resident Donnybrook mining historian and, Fred Camilleri was the grandson of the original Fred Camilleri, the prospector who pioneered the Donnybrook Goldfields with Richard Hunter in 1897. Fred (jnr) didn't make it ... not only was he virtually blind at the time, but he died at ~11am 5th April, 1996, precisely the time we were hoisting the poppet head into position. As soon as the impressive structure was raised, we committed to the tourism business plan, and 1996 became one of the busiest years of our life. We completed everything on our business plan checklist, for a planned opening on the Australia Day long weekend, January 26th 1997. About this time, a local Swiss/Australian family brought their youngest son to Australia as an immigrant. Beat worked with me in the cidery for about a year. In another beautiful life coincidence, he was a fully qualified cider maker and was invaluable in fast tracking product development. We had a full range of ciders available for sale from day one plus an apple port. The frantic days leading up to opening day were spent unloading, moving and positioning hundreds of tons of coffee rock in +40c temperatures, last minute garden landscaping.

Hilda Turnbull MLA and Hendy Cowan AO and Deputy Premier of WA, opened the Old Goldfields Orchard and Cider Factory on January 26, 1997 to a huge crowd. We gained widespread media coverage across television, state wide press, magazines and radio. Fran and Glen did all the food preparation and managed the tearooms, Russell managed the orchard and cattle while I managed the cidery, aquaculture, tours and had a part time management role in orchard. We made a good team ... so good in fact, we won the 2001 Integrated Management Award at the Telstra South West Small Business Awards. The three boys, Andrew, Dylan and Jacob were all working on the farm, the tearoom was packed, and the future looked bright. We won awards for our cider in our first year 1997, and every year thereafter, over 75 medals in total. I wrote an Excel programme specifically for the factory, which gave us total cost of production with a breakdown of raw fresh materials, glass bottle cost, cap cost, label cost, packaging cost, wages cost and inputs (variables) cost per bottle. For the first time, we had a product with control over our margins. Our daughter Hannah was working in the kitchen with Glen, and on alternate weekends Fran worked with her daughter Kate. Kate became a very capable manager in her own right. I was crushing fresh fruit, then bottling cider and fresh juice with our two sons as we wiled many hours musing over life. Space, Time, Energy and Matter have always been my thing - STEM. When I first discovered and understood that they were all manifestations of the same thing it was a revelation in understanding the law of creativity. It dawned on me that I could mould my own future and that all my dreams were simply waiting to be unlocked in time. I set up a little home recording studio and called it STEM Studios.

Eventually, one way or another, we all seem to arrive at our own understandings of the Meaning of Life. For me, life is just a gift. It can be joyful, if you want it to be. It's simple. I liken the journey and the search to the Sermon on the Mount - whatever you search for in life, will be yours. If you don't believe in anything and are always negative, you're going to get the shit kicked out of you, slammed from pillar to post, continually stumbling through life wondering what the fuck went wrong. On the contrary, if you can imagine something, then it at least becomes possible. That's when the work starts. Energy commitment. If you can't even imagine it, how can it ever be manifested? Give yourself a chance! The human brain doesn't differentiate between good and bad, it simply manifests whatever is held within it over time. If you dwell on bitterness, it will eat away at you, consume you. If you always hold hope and belief with positive conviction and, always do your best applying maximum energy into your work, everything will unfold in time. We go wrong because we don't always understand that time is our friend, an essential part of the mechanism for delivering our imagination. For me, fascination with the mind began in my teen years reading the ubiquitous Lobsang Rampa. How fucking hard did I try to levitate myself to the ceiling, so I could look down upon my body lying in bed? U.S. Anderson's book The Magic in Your Mind blew me away in 1974, before I had an epiphany in Gobbles nightclub one night, freaking Spider out with the Universal mind conversation. Ask and You Shall Receive, a book by Pierre Morency impressed me so much, I bought copies for everyone in our family. If this makes no sense to you, it doesn't really matter because, as Gerry Rafferty so succinctly put it ... "I know there ain't no special way, we all get there anyway".

Our vision of the farm at maximum potential was unfolding. I was proud of the fact we were taking our raw fresh apples to a value-added product and winning gold medals for it. Our ideas for an integrated attraction proved innovative, and we were immediately emulated by attractions further south in the Margaret River area. We looked early, at plans for an outdoor cinema but quickly dismissed the idea because our weather window was too narrow. A heritage orchard was also considered but didn't get past the final hurdle. Weekly live music over summer, blue wrens nesting in the rose garden and wedding photo ops on the lakeside boardwalk were standard offerings but, when we added an annual Cider Festival, the Backpacker Olympics and a Fishing Competition we really became the driving force behind tourism in Donnybrook at that time. We received an amazing amount of free media coverage, complementing our regular radio and local tv campaigns and we were employing up to fifty people. Actively involved in various Govt and industry working groups, we also took our business presentation on the road to various festivals and field days around the State. Working with my kids was an opportunity any father would treasure, and to this day I see it as a highlight of my thirty-seven years on the farm. We were catering for weddings, clubs, book launches, reunions, art exhibitions, corporate functions and the general public as well as regular school groups and wholesale tour bus operators. Business was booming and we headed into the new millennium feeling confident. We celebrated the millenium New Year's Eve in style, at Mick's black-tie marquee event in Eagle Bay, where we danced and partied all night long into the morning. James Paxton and I played guitar and sang for about 5 or 6 hours that night, watched the sun rise, never repeating a song.

In the cidery, 25 fruit bins (about 10,000 kilograms of apples), would yield about 5000 litres of fresh juice ready for fermentation. We had chilled stainless-steel storage for 17,000 litres. Every pressing, I'd crush enough fruit to meet total stock requirements for our range of 3 fresh juices and 5 alcoholic ciders. Hand bottling about 13,000 x 375 ml bottles of cider and ~2,000 bottles of fresh juice every batch, I could ill afford a rotator cuff injury to my right shoulder. Repetitive strain in the action of bottling caused the injury but, for the first time, I was confronted with a very real threat to my health and ability to perform tasks in the cidery. I was very worried. By the time Glen and I boarded our holiday flight to Kuching in East Malaysia/Sarawak, I could barely move my right arm. The bus trip to Damai Beach didn't help much either because on waking the next morning, I couldn't move. My back was also in agony. I managed to awkwardly make my way poolside for a massage, but no relief. The young gym attendant said he knew a guy in town who could fix me. I was desperate. We drove to "Ali's" rooms, a wooden house on stumps, not too far from the coast, with two steps leading up to the front door. Chickens were busy scratching between the rubbish piled under the house, and street kids stopped playing in the dirt and stared, as the gym attendant led Glen and I into a packed waiting room. I was curious as to how Ali could help me, but after seeing so many locals with limbs in plaster, arms in slings and people moaning and groaning, I was reassured they, at least, had confidence in him. Our gym attendant certainly did, and I felt guilty when he ushered me into Ali's room ahead of some of the others, particularly the groaning motor cycle accident victim. We'd been told Ali did not charge for his services, only accepting a donation of whatever the patient could afford. Mysteriously, we'd also been told we must take a needle on our visit. Ali was brown skinned, a tall and elderly man probably in his eighties, skinny, wearing round lens glasses and a kufi skull cap. Dressed in a loose calico caftan, he reminded me of Mahatma Gandhi. As I presented the needle, he extended his crossed, open palms and accepted it in both hands before saying a few words I didn't understand. He then placed "our" needle into a Coke bottle filled with oil, and hundreds, maybe thousands of other needles. The gym attendant, acting as our translator, explained that the oil in the bottle absorbs the energy from all Ali's other patients. Every needle represents a different patient and, the energy from every patient Ali had ever treated, was in that bottle. As I gingerly lay face down on the hard, woven grass mat, I had no idea this octogenarian had the strongest fingers and hands in the world. I honestly feared for my own health during that massage. The pain was almost unbearable and I thought I would embarrass myself and start pleading mercy. I seriously thought I had made a mistake. In between assaults, Ali replenished the oil in the bottle until eventually, he left me for dead on the floor. I lay there for some time before our gym translator gestured for me to stand up. Immediately I went to rise, I knew I had no pain at all. It was instant. I couldn't believe how good I felt. My shoulder, my back ... absolutely amazing. While I was feeling 10 years younger, Ali proceeded to assault Glen. I can't believe she endured that massage without screaming. We left a hefty donation and it's still the most amazing massage I've ever had in my life. The very next day, before lunch, the gym instructor and I climbed to the summit of Mount Santubong, a height of 810 metres, before hiking back down again for sunset beers.

A Great Sadness

Glen's father passed away on 5th August 2000 from advanced throat cancer. He had refused to allow surgeons to cut out his tongue in the months leading up to his death. He was a strong and amazing man in every sense, a wonderful husband to Nell, father to John and Charl, grandfather to many, father in law to me and Dad to Glen. She nursed him at his home until the day he died. Luckily, I was able to reiterate my promise to him that I would love and look after his little princess forever. Glen relocated her mother close by to our Donnybrook home so she could care for her, and she did - every single day. Glen had a very special relationship with her Dad, she would say he could fix anything, but Joop couldn't mend Glen's broken heart.

I forward Hannah's group text to the army: "I'm with Mum now, in HDU. Her nurse said she had a good night ... and she seems calm and comfortable. She's been breathing unassisted, just with the trachie now for more than 48hrs and looks like she is down to only 3L oxygen. Her arterial line is out now, so there are a few less tubes and cords. For a short time, she opened her eye and when I asked if she could see me she squeezed my hand, I smiled but couldn't stop the tears streaming down my face ... then a single tear ran down her cheek. I told her not to cry, that mine were happy tears knowing that she could see me, hear me and feel my hand. She has squeezed my hand a few times since and been moving her right leg quite a bit but sleeping a lot of the time. I played her a video of the girls laughing and giggling and she squeezed my hand again, to confirm she could hear them and I told her it was Addis birthday today. These fleeting moments of recognition are so special ... we just keep wishing and praying that each day they last a little longer as she recovers and regains her strength and energy xx"

I am in awe of our children.

Sunday 6th June

I wake up at 5.58am as usual but decide to try and sleep again. I open a door to a hotel room and there's Glen, standing, fully dressed. She's wearing her favourite Johnny Was jacket and mustard coloured jeans, the clothes she was wearing when this nightmare started. I realise her eyes are red but open, she's talking to me and I burst into tears - in a flash I realise it is all a dream. It's now 7.58am - the longest sleep I've had in over a month. How I wish I could hold on to that dream. Simmy, his wife Hazel and I meet for breakfast and coffee at Bayside Kitchen on the Swan River overlooking Crawley waters. Three young boys have waded through the cold, glassy water to a floating pontoon. I watch them excitedly fishing, running from creel to rod to bait board and bucket. Simmy says "I can see a young Steve Trigwell out there" ... and he's right. The innocence and naivety of youth is a gift we are only given for a short time. One day we wake up and discover it's gone, it's all been taken away. I feel like I can see all this beauty, but somehow, I'm not in all this beauty. We talk about Glen, I relate the whole story and break down again. Simmy has been very supportive throughout this ordeal. We talk about stocks, how the numbers have moved up, how the numbers have moved down ... then I wave goodbye and Simmy and Hazel drive back to my past life.

Back in St Joseph's school days, Glen, Cath and Steph were the closest of friends. Geoff, one of my housemates married Cath in December 1974, just after I'd left for Africa. Many years later, after a long battle with cancer, Geoff died a young man, with a young family. Cath asked me to play and sing at his funeral. I chose one of my own songs called Running Free, which I renamed Song for Geoff. I decide to send her a text: "Hi Cathy. I'm not sure if you have heard any reports on Glen's health. Maybe I should have text you earlier but was a little worried your Mum might not handle the news too well. We have had a tough time since March 26th. Glen was diagnosed with a brain aneurysm which was operated on within 24 hrs, but worsened after a stent insertion proved ineffective. Neuro surgeons operated to do an arterial bypass, it too failed. They re-did the bypass with a new vein taken from her right leg. The second bypass failed also. Glen had a stroke right then. After a few days, pressure began building in her head and they went in again performing a decompression craniectomy ... removing a section of skull to relieve pressure. Glen has not woken up since the first bypass was done on 18th May. Sorry to drop all this on you Cath ... but I know how close you, Steph and Glen were in school days and later. God bless you. Steve". Cath responds ... she knew. The army has grown, beyond my knowledge. It's Addi's third birthday so I quickly face time Dylan and Karlee, Addi is excited about her visit to the playground, her new "Frozen" shoes and a life size cardboard cut-out of Moana. I make my way to the hospital, where I know Hannah is sitting with Glen. I was hoping for a miracle on June 6th, but that's ok, I can wait.

Our lives and the farm business changed forever on Nov 20th 2001, when Russell's wife Fran passed away, at her home on the farm, after a long fight with cancer. We were all devastated, no-one more so than Russell and his two children Kate and Andrew. I am sure Fran's death prompted Russ to pause and re-evaluate his life. He was a lost soul for many months and it was sad to see. He found comfort spending more time on weekends with his kids, close friends and watching his son Andrew's hockey and Dockers football. He also became more active in a horse racing syndicate with some close buddies. I now know what he was going through, and realise the support he received and needed from his friends was invaluable. He was thrust, overnight, into a different reality, a different world. It was a very tough time for Russ, and a very difficult time on the farm. Russ never remarried and struggled for a long time adjusting to life without Fran. We all tried desperately to keep the farm moving forward. By now Russ was in his early fifties and our permanent orchard staff including long time employees Bob and Martin, as well as Andrew, Dylan and for a short time Jake, were doing the heavy lifting in the field with Russ copping jibes like "he's allergic to the picking bag". Eventually, Bob left for a job off farm and the boys all gravitated to the big money in the mining industry and who could blame them. Glen was still hurting from losing her Dad but, for a short time assumed a bigger role in the tearooms, reducing her shift work nursing in Bunbury, trying to fill the gap left with Fran's passing. It wasn't long though, before the extra workload took its toll on Glen and I truly believe she was close to a mental breakdown.

The first chinks in Glen's health were beginning to emerge, with stress, sore feet and fatigue. Eventually, we appointed a manager and hired extra staff to operate the business without Fran, Glen or Kate at the coal face. For the first time, we didn't have any business owner working the tearooms.

While we were formulating a new strategy in the tearooms, our interactive website and online shop was working well. Our database was expanding via the cellar door, but I found myself living a life I didn't enjoy. Around this time, we were audited by the ATO or Australian Taxation Office, Federal Excise Division. Officers Terry Morgan and Steve Visser made multiple visits and numerous investigations into so called excise duty evasion but we were, in the end, totally exonerated. As a producer, I was forced to increase the alcohol content of our ciders from 3.5% to 8.1% allowing them to be classified as fruit wines, to be eligible for the same taxation concessions as wine producers. The investigation took two years, reams of correspondence with Government bureaucrats Mitch Fifield and Phillip Gaetgens and, a purported meeting with Federal Treasurer Peter Costello. Held at the Italian Club in White Street Bunbury, the proposed meeting was nothing more than a party fundraiser, where I was seated next to Mitch Fifield and, Costello appeared to be drunk the entire time. Implementation of the new tax system on cideries was either a bureaucratic bungle of the highest order, or a clever piece of lobbying by Bulmers and other national producers who never had a cellar door. The investigation eventually concluded the Government had made errors in the implementation of ANTS, or A New Tax System, better known as the GST. Two words ... "and cider" ... had been omitted from the refund side of the legislation. After a 2-year battle and eventual representation by Geoff Prosser MP, the laws were finally changed and corrected to include "and cider". ATO officers Morgan and Visser informed us we were the test case for the whole of Australia, because their records showed we were the first boutique cidery in the nation. Another cidery opened in Bridgetown about 12 months after us and, eventually, others began in the hills surrounding Perth. Within a few years cideries were everywhere, nationally, including Tasmania. I'm sure all those cideries are totally unaware Old Goldfields fought a two-year tax battle, arguing with the Federal Govt to finally get the taxation laws changed to treat cidery cellar doors the same as wineries. By the time the audit was over I had grey hair and had totally lost faith in Govt.

I get a text from Mal: "Mate, when you are ready we will have a play. We were going to have a jam over the next month or so, to get tight for when you are ready. When you feel you are up to it, let us know. Love you both". I respond: "Mal if Glen doesn't pull through this I'm not sure I'll still be playing. I've been so fortunate to have had the opportunity to surround myself with 3 great musos (u guys) .... but musically, I don't feel like I've got much else to say now and I've always felt that I only ever sang for her anyway. That may change of course but right now I am feeling pretty uninspired. Sorry mate ..."

Mon 7th June

La Galette is closed. No coffee - I'm pissed, then I remember it's a public holiday, oh well. No big changes with Glen so I send this text to the kids: "I'm in with Mum now ... she is peacefully sleeping. I gently held her hand and spoke to her for a while but no response so I'm going to sit here and wait for a wriggle or arm movement. All good."

My own Dad passed away on 10th June 2004. Glen helped nurse him at home when she could, in between caring for her own Mum. Dad was an imposing figure, a sporting ruckman in his day and a champion at every sport he turned his hand to. He played in 11 football finals series including 9 grand finals. Winning 8 of them, they lost the 1952 Grand Final by 2 points. He was voted best and fairest 9 years in a row, and for 7 of those years he played off in the GF. He played league football for South Fremantle aged 16, during the war years. At various stages of his life, he was either club champion or simply excelled at golf, tennis and lawn bowls. From personal experience, I can vouch for his prowess in darts and 8 ball. He and our Mum married in 1949. Following a failed attempt at working alongside his own father on the farm, he joined the police force. In her late seventies, Mum wrote her life story in a book called Both Sides of The Coin. She detailed how even a generation prior, our grandad Syd couldn't generate enough farm income to sustain himself and his wife, 2 sons with growing families and a third son, who never married. Eventually, after banking profits from the wool price boom in the early 1950's, Syd split the farm, giving 2 sons roughly half the land each, and making a substantial cash payout to the third son. All three sons were to find jobs and careers off farm. Our grandad lived on the farm until needing permanent care, eventually passing away in a Donnybrook aged care facility aged 92, in 1979. That succession plan created deep divisions and resulted in such a waste of potential brotherly love.

My Dad was a complex character. He deeply loved Mum and all of us and was very proud of his family and heritage, but he did not show his emotions easily. He wasn't the Dad who would wrap his arms around you. His idea of strength, was to not show weakness. He was a perfectionist in doing things his way. Mum was a feminist before her time, never took a backward step and staunchly defended her hard-won independence. As a consequence, our parents spent a lifetime arguing over mundane, insignificant forgetables. Mum always said 21 years as a policeman hardened him to survive. As a kid, I can remember him attending road accidents, suicides and brawls, and on one occasion we had a woman at our front door with a machete in her back. Dad softened after he retired, when he no longer saw himself as the protector, defender and provider. Mum always said he mellowed with age. In a rare moment of vulnerability, I saw Dad actually shed a tear once, before he quickly turned away. We were walking together, the Old Goldfields Orchard and Cider Factory was booming, pumping at its peak ... and as we walked amongst the crowd he commented, "I wish your grandad could see this place now". Dad was a very popular man when he quit the police force. The Brunswick townsfolk threw a going away party as a thank you gesture and 300 people turned up. Even the drunks and crooks were there. I can still hear his raucous laugh ... and I miss him. At his funeral Mum played "My Way" by Frank Sinatra, I wonder if they argued about that selection?

Western Australia was going through a mining and commodities boom in the years leading up to the GFC in 2007. Residential house prices were rising rapidly and both Russell and I had bought properties in Bunbury in 2005. By now our daughter Hannah was living in Perth working as a nurse and, Russell's daughter Kate was helping out in the tearooms in between being busy as a young mother. All three boys were either already working off farm or about to leave, building their own careers. Andrew took a mature age apprenticeship working at Worsley, Dylan began working on an offshore oil rig and Jake became a qualified fitter machinist FIFO working in the Pilbara. With Fran gone, and Russ, Glen and myself falling out of love with the farm, Old Goldfields was like a ship without a rudder. The succession of managers we installed in the tearooms never attained the level of success enjoyed by Fran and Glen and we had begun pushing out fruit trees.

Mal and Av meet me for lunch at the cafe on the ground floor of the Children's Hospital. So many people want to help, but there is nothing anyone can do - except pray. I ask Mal how old he is ... 51 years. I feel like an old man. I've been playing music with him since he was about 17 years old. Hannah has been asking when is Pa going to come and stay with Marley in their house in Embleton. Mick and Tracey insist I can stay with them in Peppy Grove for as long as I like but, I just have no idea what the fuck I am doing really. I'm a 67-year-old couch surfer but I think maybe I can be of help to Hannah. We are all doing it tough at the moment and she has two little kids and a husband at work. I let Mick know my plans, pack my bag and we meet Tracey for coffee in Cottesloe. As I'm leaving I shed a tear and tell him ... "make sure you pull the zip up mate".

Tues 8th June

"I've been in with Mum for a while now. No change essentially. All good. I asked to see the doctor, the physio and the OT just to get my head around status and what can I do now etc. Dr will see me later, but physio and speech pathologist are with her now. They are testing the balloon pressure around the trachie to see if Glen can swallow and cough properly. This is the pathway for eventual trachie reversal if she meets the criteria." I'm trying to remain positive but fuck it's hard. I shed another tear as I sit beside her thinking if it's hard for me, how hard must it be for her? Bronte the nurse from Australind is fantastic, but I keep thinking how can this be happening?

Stephen Trigwell

The Beginning of the End

I had already proposed to Russell that we sell the farm but in the early days he wouldn't hear of it so we soldiered on. After returning from a week holiday in Bali, Glen and I were confronted by a disturbing email. It seems while we were away, Kate's de facto partner had decided to slaughter some live sheep in the yards adjacent to the tearooms. It was an abhorrent act apparently committed in front of tourists, including children. I never, ever forgave him for that. To this day I can't believe he was unaware or ignorant of what he was doing. It must have been a deliberate act, I just don't know why.

A prominent investor came to us with a proposal to develop a part of our property, including building about 300 residences with some aged care homes and a caravan park. I agreed to make a clean break, sell my half of the farm to the developer, and walk away. We struck a handshake agreement on the price for our share, and the plan was Russell and he together would progress the development as a joint venture. Russell asked me not to sell my share immediately, rather wait on the approvals process first. I agreed. The developer planned on bringing sewerage and piped scheme water five kilometres from Donnybrook to the farm. The plan included roads, public open space, drainage, kerbing, lighting etc. At considerable cost, we employed a tourism consultant to compile a research report into the proposal. At this point, I realised in my naivety I had agreed to "a call" over my share of the property, at a price greatly below what it would have been worth once all approvals were granted. It was an unintended consequence on my part of the developer not buying our share outright, as I had envisaged. I guess that's why he was the developer and I was the cider maker! The Dept of Planning and Infrastructure approved a highly modified plan which didn't suit the developer entirely, but eventually, the shire knocked back the application anyway and the whole proposal fell over. Other private proposals for caravan parks in Donnybrook were routinely knocked back until finally, the shire proceeded to build their own caravan park and also subdivide shire land for residential and aged care homes. The shire then proposed building a museum in the town of Donnybrook and asked us if we would like to donate any paraphernalia from our own museum. By this stage, I'm beginning to feel like we are in competition with local govt. A workshop was called for in the local town hall, asking residents to bring their ideas and visions for the town. I proposed a couple of initiatives. Because it was so cold, I thought turning Donnybrook into the "deciduous capital" of the south west was an easy option. Secondly, having visited Montville, a known artists "hotspot" in Queensland, I was impressed with a waterwheel I'd seen there and, how they'd opened up buildings, allowing tourists to stroll between shops without resorting to the footpath. I suggested a massive working waterwheel at the northern entrance to Donnybrook, on the Noneycup Creek opposite the Anchor and Hope Inn, to be built over a neat stone or concrete dam wall holding back a "Monet" style garden pond. Clever ground and up-lighting could turn the surrounding lawn and gardens, and indeed the wheel itself, into a magical night time fairyland where families could meet. Such an entrance statement would "brand" the town as unique, make a great photo opportunity, and if done right, be quite beautiful. To the shire's credit, they did plant deciduous trees. Alas, the waterwheel did not get the nod, neither did the retail makeover. Much later however, the shire suggested the boat Australia 11 be relocated to Donnybrook as a tourist attraction. Really? Donnybrook has no ocean. The town itself is not even on the coast. As far as I am aware there is no link whatsoever between Donnybrook and Australia II.

Things went from bad to worse in mid 2008, when Russ fell off a mechanical platform while pruning fruit trees. He broke his neck, was placed in a neck brace for months and was extremely lucky not to have been made quadriplegic from the neck down. One day, standing in his neck brace, Russ was observing as I pushed cows through a raceway to be loaded onto a truck for sale. Suddenly, one of the cows turned and my left leg was trapped, twisted and crushed against the railing, damaging my left knee. I fell to the concrete floor of the cattle yards in pain, sat in the cow shit and nearly passed out. After about 5 minutes I tested the knee but it was like rubber, I had no control over my leg below the knee. I dragged myself through the shit and sat on an inverted half drum, while Russ rang Glen to come and take me to hospital. I ended up with my anterior cruciate, lateral collateral, and medial collateral ligaments smashed, with a deep vein thrombosis (clot) in my leg. Sitting in a lounge chair with my left leg raised and my knee on ice, I watched the entire 2008 Beijing Olympics. I never realised how boring archery and trap shooting were until then, and every time they crossed to the badminton or table tennis there was no game on at all - that was a blessing.

I was still wearing the full leg/knee brace when Glen decided to take her Mum to a reunion in Mount Ida, north west of Kalgoorlie. We caught the Prospector train from Perth and enjoyed a dinner function with all the ex-residents, before taking a convoy of buses 242 kilometres to the gold mining ghost town. Joop and Nell had spent their early married years there when the town was bustling. Joop was an electrician on the mine, often working underground. As a voyeur at the reunion it was a surreal feeling watching the ex-townsfolks' memories come alive. Where I saw a dusty track, they saw a bustling street named the Straight Eight. Where I saw a small, broken concrete slab, the old timers argued over rooms in a magnificent, invisible house. Where they saw the kids jumping the fence and playing in the one room primary school yard ... I saw a circle of stones and a lone tree.

In September 2009 I received a phone call from Tanya Imhoff. Her father, my old boss Gerd had passed away August 17th in Vancouver, Canada aged 67. I felt a great loss. I was honoured to have known him, and even more privileged to think Tanya took the time to call me. For just a moment, I recalled when Gerd and Christine took me to see World Safari by Alby Mangels, Aussie adventurer, at a suburban hall in Richmond, Vancouver. Gerd was a dreamer and an adventurer, I think that's why we got on so well.

We searched for the perfect manager in the tearooms, but the perfect manager was gone and Glen was burnt out and exhausted, so we devised another plan. We decided to sell our cattle herd, agist (rent) the pastures, lease out the orchard and lease out the cidery and tourism side of the business. By 2010, all lease agreements had been drawn up by our solicitor, signed and implemented. Cattle agistment was a periodic lease over a defined land area, the tourism lease covered the restaurant and cider factory and the orchard lease included access to water rights from several large dams. Basically, we downsized our working commitments in exchange for becoming landlords. For the first time in decades, we had time to spare so, when Johnny rang with the Abrolhos fishing trip offer, I grabbed it. Glen was supportive of me taking "bloke time" and, for the next decade I'd spend between a week and a month on John's boat Ocean Spirit, enjoying the amazing Abrolhos Archipelago every Easter/Anzac period. The Anzac dawn service on Big Pidgeon island is quite special, however the "two up" school on West Wallaby Island, immediately following the service is famous, a slice of real Australiana and deserving of its iconic reputation. Pristine coral reefs link the remote 125-kilometre chain of low-lying limestone islands, home to a unique rock lobster fishing industry, pearl farming and eco-tourism. As kids growing up in Brunswick, Johnny and I learnt guitar together and, as he knew a few pro fishermen, Johnny and the Magnums became regular entertainers at Macca's hut on Big Pidgeon island. The annual Macca's hut concert was a stone's throw from the scene of the infamous and shameful 4th June 1629 Batavia mutiny and subsequent massacre. Some of the historical stone "fortress" is still visible today.

Physio is again testing Glen off the trachie ... she does 11 minutes. Apparently, that's good as some only do 30 secs at the start. Any good news is a positive. The Doctor is worried Glen's heart rate is too high so they order a scan at 7.00pm. A bureaucratic blunder delays the scan, but after 4 attempts the junior Doctor finally gets the cannula in the vein. I can't believe this is happening to my wife. Dylan and I drive back to Hannah's house. At 8.55pm I get a call from the dreaded unknown number. Glen has got a blood clot in her left lung. For fucks sake - what else can go wrong?

Glen and I had been to Africa in 2006 with all 3 kids and had an amazing family holiday so, in early 2010, I decided to set myself the goal of climbing Kilimanjaro as the final challenge in my knee rehabilitation. Dylan and Jake were immediately keen to join me, then once my nephew Andrew heard about our plans he wanted in on the challenge. Not wanting to let the young guns down, I trained 4 or 5 days a week in the gym for about 6 months before we began the trek in August 2010. Jake's preparation consisted of running up the Bunbury maidens sandhill once, the weekend before we left. He didn't want to over train. We spent 9 days on the mountain trekking the Machame route, reaching the summit on August 19th. It's a memory I'll never forget, and to do it with the three boys was a gift from God. As we camped atop the Barranco Wall, on the final night before our assault on the summit, the wind was fierce, blowing against the 257-metre cliff face that was the Barranco. A so-called bio loo, with a round hole in the floor had been built on the edge of the cliff. Don't ask me where the wee and poo ended up, I have no idea. As I wiped my arse and shoved the paper down the hole, the wind blew it straight back at me and this piece of shit laden paper was flying around the room in a vortex, like a swooping magpie. After somehow escaping the shitbox I slept, before waking at 4am to join the snake of head torches winding through the pitch black, reaching Uhuru Peak, 5895 metres above sea level at sunrise. We finished the holiday with a week in Zanzibar, where I wanted to renew our wedding vows. I always felt Glen deserved a more romantic proposal than the one she got in 1981. She wouldn't hear of it ... happy with the old ones, but I did give her the new vows I wrote on the mountain on the day of our anniversary, the 14th August. Glen and I flew home via Singapore, attending a wedding on Sentosa Island. The boys stayed in Africa and bungee jumped off the Stormsvlei Bridge, the highest land-based bungee in the world at the time. They must have gotten a taste for heights because as soon as we returned to Australia, they talked me into jumping out of a plane at 12,000 feet. They got me at a weak moment.

The neighbouring farmer had leased our orchard and quickly proceeded to convert it to organic production techniques. It was a bold and promising move, but over time the trees began to decline. Russ was asked by the lessee to work with him as a paid employee. He agreed, as did I at a later date. The day we signed the tourism/cider lease, and before the ink had dried, our tenant said "oh I can't pay the rent in advance I'll have to pay in arrears at the end of the month". So began my 5-year apprentice as a commercial lawyer. Our solicitor had drawn up an iron clad lease agreement, by the end of the first 5 years I knew every clause. I would spend hours painstakingly constructing legalese emails before Glen would proof read it and say "you can't say that" or "you'd be better off saying it this way". I would stay up past midnight, agonising over choice of words, then show her the end result in the morning and she'd say "no you're better off just ignoring that, you don't need to respond". By now, Russell was living in his Bunbury unit and driving to and from Donnybrook, working for our orchard tenant. Glen and I were still living in Boulder Street but she had resigned as a midwife and was working part time at the local aged care facility and caring for her mother. I was sending out three invoices a month ... but reconciling and chasing up constant legal issues with the tourism/cider tenant was driving me crazy and taking up a lot of my time.

The doctor orders another scan to work out where Glen's lung clot came from. We're initially devastated to learn she has DVT's in both legs, before they assure us the issue is common in long term bedridden patients and the treatment is effective and relatively non-invasive. They start her on a low dose of Heparin and will consider a blood filter under close monitoring.

By the end of 2010 Glen was nursing her mother full time and regularly sleeping overnight in Nell's independent aged care apartment. Nell suffered a fall, and was admitted to Donnybrook Hospital where the local catholic priest was called to administer the last rites. Nell was motionless, pale and silent as she lay on the bed. It was a scene from a movie as the priest went about the ancient ritual before shuffling out slowly while we sat in silence. Suddenly, Nell opened her eyes and began chatting, like it was a second coming, nothing had happened and she was ready to party! She returned home for a few weeks, before finally allowing Glen to arrange for her transfer into a high care facility. Her admittance was organised for Thursday 17th February 2011 at 12 noon. She died that morning. It's a strange feeling when the last of your own parents passes away. Glen was philosophical and stoic, as she'd had some time to prepare but, she was still very upset and saddened. For me, losing my parents was a feeling of loneliness and emptiness. For the first time in my life, I didn't have any parents. I was an orphan. Suddenly, I felt so much older. It took me a long while to find my new place in the Universe. I know Glen felt the same.

Russell agreed to sell the farm and, although his idea of the realisable value was higher than mine, we decided to test the market and listed it at his higher price. We had a few tyre kickers come through, but no offers and no serious interest. The real estate market continued to decline but even after a price drop we received no offers. Glen had been having trouble with her feet for many years, but continually dismissed the pain as being caused by long periods standing while nursing, or ill-fitting shoes. In late 2013 Glen collapsed in agony; she spent a week in hospital and was diagnosed with rheumatoid arthritis or RA. She was devastated. Initially in hospital for a week, the insidious disease gradually had a huge impact on her life. She had to give up work immediately and went into a pain and drug treatment programme. When first diagnosed, she researched RA and went on an incredibly strict diet. Distraught when it didn't reverse the disease, we booked a trip to Bali, leaving no stone unturned in a quest to reverse her RA nightmare. We travelled to Ubud and arranged a meeting with a respected holy man. The idea that ancient cultures and beliefs are devoid of truth and therefore should be dismissed, was folly to both of us. Traditions and belief systems survive because people believe in them. Whether that belief is founded upon sand is just somebody's opinion really, totally irrelevant, because truth always survives. We booked for a week at White Lotus villas off Jalan Kajeng and awaited the holy man visit. Wayan came and went, in a deeply spiritual encounter Glen was moved but, ultimately not cured - maybe we just didn't believe hard enough? Unfortunately, it took about 2 years and a change of specialists before an effective pain management regime was arrived at. Glen's life had changed forever, but she never once lost her enthusiasm, zest for life or sense of humour. She was always mindful and grateful for the many blessings we enjoyed.

Our attempts to attract a buyer for the farm were unsuccessful. We decided to change real estate agents, with the new agent suggesting a "silent listing" to be followed by an auction to try and flush out any interested parties. The neighbouring farmers, one of whom was a tenant, were considered likely bidders and both attended the auction on 10th November 2013. It was the morning of my 60th birthday and I was hoping for a successful result. Some lively bidding was had, but the price never reached the reserve, indicating our price was still north of tempting a successful bid. We had at least determined where the market wasn't! Glen and I had previously invited our friends and relatives to a planned birthday celebration at the Berry Delightful

Tearooms about 10 kilometres south of Donnybrook. We were of course, hoping it would have also been a celebration of a successful auction. Good friends Marc and Sarah have spent a lifetime realising their dream of a unique, almost spiritual venue, surrounded by magnificent exotic gardens, water features, light and shade and a hillside with 1,000 rose bushes. Stickfish reformed for the gig and we opened up with You Can't Always Get What You Want by the Stones, with cameos from Johnny Wenc on lead guitar and Alan Payne on keyboards. We lowered our toy version of Stonehenge from the leafy canopy above, right onto Mal as he played ... a tribute to Spinal Tap the Movie. The blow-up doll with microphone in her mouth was my idea, I had been threatening to do it as a stage act for years - just didn't want to leave that stunt undone. My Mum enjoyed the afternoon immensely. In a short speech, I made special mention that it was her who first encouraged me into music at fourteen years of age, buying me my first Yamaha acoustic guitar for $10 from Musgroves music shop in Bunbury. I think she was chuffed.

My Mum, Pam Trigwell, wrote her life story, Both Sides of The Coin when she was 79-80 years of age. Her own mother died a methylated spirit alcoholic when Mum was 9 years old. Her father was dead by the time she was 13. She had a tragic childhood, separated from her only brother and moving between 21 foster homes over a 5-year period. My Dad's parents didn't like Pam at all, thought she was an interloper and tried to dissuade her from marrying their son. They refused to pay for any part of the wedding, eventually enough friction built for my Dad to leave the farm and become a policeman. Mum was a very independent, strong willed, smart and capable woman, but her overarching purpose in life was always to foster love within her family unit. She wanted a home where love was limitless, constant and free, just like the one she never had. She succeeded. She defended her three boys like a lioness, always offering unconditional love and support, giving each of us every chance she could, including buying me a $10 guitar. After Dad died, Mum went about realising her dream of becoming an accomplished artist, before a fall in 2015 resulted in her being admitted into high care after a stroke. She was well aware we were selling the farm, and supportive of the plan. They confiscated her electric wheelchair for speeding in the corridors, just before she passed away on May 1st, 2016.

After a few prospective buyer inspections met with disinterest, our agent suggested the farmhouse was weighing negatively on buyer sentiment. Apparently, some potential buyers liked the property but the farmhouse itself was unacceptable. We took a drive and inspected the house. I was shocked. The inside of the building was in disrepair and our farmhouse tenant, constantly behind in paying his rent, had trashed the place. Glen had a bold idea. She suggested we sell our Boulder Street house, move into the farmhouse and completely renovate it, to facilitate a sale. I agreed on the condition that we had an acceptable farm budget allocation to complete the renovation, and that we actually dropped our asking price to meaningfully meet the market. Russ agreed. A local real estate agent appraised our Boulder Street house at $385k. The market was weak, but the house was in an excellent location and presented well. We asked $425k, but after one offer quickly fell through, it sold for the exact appraisal value with a short settlement date. We had already given the farmhouse tenant notice to move out by Valentine's Day 2016. The settlement on our Boulder Street house was March 9th 2016. Glen and I had already pre-booked a trip to Sydney and Queensland, so we had 23 days in which to complete the entire renovation before departure. The house was structurally sound but showing age. It was a 1970's style, dark brick home with a colorbond metal roof and open plan design. We set about prioritising the tasks, arranging tradesmen if necessary and ordering materials. Glen and I worked every day from 5 or 6am until 11 or 12 midnight for the entire 23 days straight. Our first priority was to completely renovate two bathrooms. I contacted a local tiler who kindly loaned me his percussion jack hammer and I set about removing a bath and all the old tiles, in preparation for him to lay new ones. We fitted new hand basins and toilet pedestals as well as a new bath, new glass shower screens, fixtures, tap ware, lighting and mirrors. Many of the interior house walls were dark face brick so we replaced them with gyprock panels to lighten the space. We tore up the original 37-year-old tattered floor coverings and laid new throughout. Pulling out the ageing stove, freezer and fridge, laying new kitchen bench tops and fitting all new appliances gave the kitchen a fresh, bright, pristine look. The house was starting to look fantastic and a complete interior paint job, together with all new window treatments and light fittings topped it off. Glen and Hannah chose light, fresh, neutral colours and were creative in white-lime washing the dark, face brick entry, using a mirror and plants to give it a spacious and bright feel. We had converted one small bedroom into an office as well as re-invented the outdoor garden and terraced outlook across pastures to the dam. Some paving maintenance and new outdoor light fittings, followed by an exterior high pressure clean finished the renovations. We curved a garden pathway leading to a bright yellow entrance gate, where we hung a small bell. The makeover was complete. The house had been brought into the 21st Century in 23 days, for about $23k. It looked fantastic. Why the hell hadn't we done it before?

Wed 9th June

Glen fasted all day today as the doctors have decided to push ahead with the blood filter op. They intend going in through the groin and chasing an "umbrella" type filter up into the vena cava vein to protect the heart and lungs from blood clots should any more dislodge from the DVT's in the legs. Unfortunately, the op gets delayed due to an emergency situation with other patients. They put Glen back on a nasogastric tube nutrition feed overnight.

Thurs 10th June

A breakthrough day, I send this text to the kids: "Traffic terrible today ... had to wait ages for a car park too. In with Mum now ... best day so far. Physio was here when I arrived and Mum had both eyes open before closing right eye. 15 minutes off trachie and they put a little gadget on it - through which she tried to voice. They said she was trying to say hi ... it's a start. Apparently, she initiated a few swallows but cannot measure the strength of that yet. She squeezed my hand, as well as held her hand to her mouth and blew me a kiss (tiny lip purse) at the request of the physio. She also waved goodbye (raised hand and twinkled fingers), 3 times to the nurse and physio on request, as they left. Mum moving her right leg and right arm in seemingly purposeful movements right now - almost like she is exercising. Wow ... exciting. Even the speech therapist had a tear in her eye. Tracey and Helen, the nurses, are so caring and lively... I know Glen would love them". To make a good day even better, Glen's brother John has flown in from Northern New South Wales. Glen is really happy to see him as she squeezes his hand. John sheds a tear when she complies to his request to twinkle her fingers and wave at him. He's booked a motel close by the hospital, intending to walk every day to sit by her side. He'll be here for a week. John is a very positive guy and doesn't accept or entertain negative so it will be great having him around. Glen has been fasting all day for the filter op but delayed again. Bugger.

Fri 11th June

I'm at HDU by 10am, meet John and we both sit with Glen for a while. We can see Glen is trying to smile, even a hint of a chuckle as John relates stories to Glen. At 1pm I drive to Claremont Quarter and buy some nice moisturisers for Glen, as well as spoil her with some Bottega Veneta perfume and body lotion. Together with the creams and lotions she has collected in "get well" hampers she will have the softest skin in HDU. While I'm there I notice one of my tyres is losing air so I drop into Tyrepower - young Ben fixes it but won't take any payment. "Drop me in a six pack if you insist". God, I love this country and its people. Glen finally gets back from having the blood filter fitted. She had again been fasting all morning so I was pleased it wasn't delayed again. Mary and Alistair are back from Queensland and at about 4pm, Mary is in tears as Glen twinkle waves at her. I can't believe that after 2 days fasting, physio, trachie test work and the filter op she is still even awake. A big sleep tonight will do her good. I pop to the Albion for one quick beer and a couple of "non-alcoholics" with the boys. While I'm there, I donate $10 in a breast cancer raffle and win a huge meat hamper. Things are turning around! We are winning. Back in HDU by 7pm, I tell Glen the good news about the hamper and she gets the happy smirk again. Nice. Dylan asks Glen to give John a peace sign and she holds up two fingers in the familiar V. Then he asks for the rock n roll sign, she holds up the thumb and pinkie. Finally, he asks her to give John the *middle finger and she does! Everybody laughs, Glen gets the little smirk. She's back folks! Now we start the long road to a recovery. We all drive to Greenwood and watch Chris's daughter Ellie play football. It's been another good day.*

We flew to Sydney the day after we finished the renovations on the farmhouse. Enroute to the airport and driving through Argyle, 8 kilometres north of Donnybrook, I had a very strange feeling come over me. Glen and I were discussing whether we had the energy to undertake another house renovation. I suddenly felt there was something very important I would need to do sometime in the future, not necessarily a house renovation, just some unfinished business in my life. I had no idea what the future held for me but, in the spirit of embracing feelings of uncertainty, I wasn't daunted, and remember feeling anticipation tinged with excitement.

We'd always loved Sydney and had been there many times, but I had never been to an opera at the Opera House. In all the times we'd walked around and inside the famous and amazing building, I had never ticked it off my bucket list to actually attend an opera. We booked into an old restored 19th century hotel in The Rocks area, walking distance to the Opera House. As Glen dressed, upstairs, I followed the rabbit warren of corridors, took a narrow staircase downstairs and wandered into the front bar. There were two guys sitting apart, their shoes resting on the brass foot rail. I sat in the middle and ordered a pint. Maybe it was the old original surrounds, maybe it was the friendly chat with total strangers, maybe it was the ghosts of the early settlers - but I was filled with a feeling of arrival, a comfortable feeling like ... this was home. I felt like I was a part of history and I was doing what I had to do.

Glen and I meandered down through Nurses Walk, past The Fortune of War hotel and on past bustling Circular Quay and the ferries. We strolled toward the most iconic building in Australia and marvelled, as the Sydney harbour bridge hung there in all its magnificence. La Boheme was stupendous, and Glen played Julia Roberts to a tee. During interval, I stepped outside, leaned against a wall and wrote:

"So here I am at the Opera House, it wasn't always this way. There were decades old blisters and buckets of sweat, family feuds and the stench of regret. I've finally arrived, swell in my finery. Is this the dream? Am I the dream? Is this what you imagined or, did you dream for more? What if I never arrived, would I have failed you? Would you have berated me? I can hear you, I can see you. The ghost of Henry dancing on the cobblestones, clickety clack, clickety clack, clickety. Gaslights flicker, and the London fog turns to black. They all hurry, they're going to the opera. Everyone hurries, we're all going to the opera".

Before leaving Sydney, we took the ferry to Manly and strolled the shops. Afterwards we walked, way down by the jetty landing, where the pontoons bump and sway, the others read and standing, as the Manly ferry cuts its way to Circular Quay. Because we could.

Glen and I only lived in the farmhouse for a year before we sold the farm to a couple from Graaff-Reinet, near Port Elizabeth in South Africa. Back in 1975 I hitch hiked through Graaff-Reinet - it was Karoo country, on the Eastern Cape, dry and relatively barren. Roy and Jenny spent months, searching Australia wide for a property with reliable rainfall, eventually emigrating their entire family for a new life in a new land, just as Henry Trigwell had done 165 years before. I love how the world turns in circles. Russell believed our eventual selling price was too low - 3 years had passed since the unsuccessful auction, and real estate prices had continued to decline. I was more than happy with the price and relieved to be able to start a new stage in our lives. The reality was - "it is what it is". The market had spoken and determined the price.

Stephen Trigwell

At Last the Golden Years

Immediately after the farm sold, Glen and I moved into our Bunbury town house in Symmons Street. We'd bought the place in 2005 when, on a drive along the beach near Wyalup, Glen pointed to the block of 5 town houses and said "I've always wanted to live there". Her Dad had fished the black basalt ledges at Rocky Point for as long as she could remember, so when she spotted a "Private Sale" sign on the balcony window she immediately called the number. Within an hour we had inspected the house and our offer had been accepted. We rented it out for 12 years, occasionally grabbing a week or two holiday in between tenants. Every time we drove past Glen would say "if I never get to live there, make sure you drive my hearse past on the way to the cemetery". My Mum told me we needed to sell the farm before we lost our Golden Years. I wasn't exactly sure what "Golden Years" was, but we never lost sight of our vision to live by the sea and, when 2017 became our year, we finally discovered Mum's Golden Years - she was right, as usual. She knew Glen had rheumatoid arthritis and, for some time I'd felt something else wasn't quite right with Glen's health. I was grateful to be able to spend all my time by her side.

From our balcony, we can watch the sun rise over the familiar Darling Ranges in the east. I know those hills well, having spent my childhood on the banks of the Brunswick River. Looking north, the black and white checked lighthouse stands like a sentinel, overlooking "our playing field" where the boys in white play their cricket and, when in a particularly masochistic mood, I might run a lap or two. In the west, the watery diamond droplets shine silver and gold on the black rocks as the sun slowly sinks into the Indian Ocean. Every afternoon in summer, we stroll the short walk to the beach, and take the same photos of the same but, different beauty. Glen always goes barefoot to feel the sand between her toes. The colours are never the same. The reflections are never quite the same. On occasion, if I'm in the mood, I'll take the guitar and sing a song or two. If I can find a quiet spot it's always kind of nice, although usually guaranteed to meet an ear. At other times, the thought is anathema as it feels like an imposition on what is such natural beauty.

After we sold the farm I finally had some funds with which to invest. I'd been trading options and equities for years, albeit with limited capital and with varying levels of success. In my early years of investing, Dylan and I would trade together. He started collecting company reports in primary school, graduated to buying stocks, then found an appetite for buying and selling puts and calls throughout high school. Glen always referred to him by his initials DJT. One night we sat around the desktop until way past midnight, watching pink slips trade on the OTC market in New York. I took to managing our retirement finances with enthusiasm, conscious of our need to diversify our risk profile at the same time as generate income. I spent about 6 months researching whatever I thought was important, all the while keeping the bulk of our liquid assets in either cash or relatively conservative income yielding investments. The day the farm funds settled, I made an early allocation into various crypto currencies as I'd been following their emergence and sensed an opportunity. As time went by, I began to focus more on global macro trends, opportunity sectors, ASX micro and small caps as well as getting my head around basic technical analysis. I found I loved the liquidity of the markets, enabling me to be a nimble investor, making instant decisions on whether to be in an industry, company sector or not - something which is impossible as a farmer. A trend on the ASX could be 2 weeks, a trend on the farm could be 2-5 years, a trend in crypto could be two minutes.

After 12 years of renting, the town house was looking a bit tired and we were fired up to renovate again. The plan was to convert an unused rear balcony space into a main bedroom ensuite. Clever design meant we ended up with a walk-in pantry as well. We contracted a builder to complete the renovation while we began to excitedly plan a trip to Canada to visit our youngest son Jake, who was working the ski fields in Jasper. We actually had no real intention of going to Canada, until Glen made another of her whimsical decisions. After receiving a text on her phone advertising return tickets to San Francisco for $950, she booked two. Stocks were booming so we dived into holiday planning with gusto, turning our Jasper sojourn into a dream holiday.

Sat 12th June

I send out this text: "Hi everybody ... sorry about group text but easier. Glen had another good day today, waving fingers and hand on right side. Right hand to mouth ok, scratching top lip with right hand. Still very tired from insertion of a blood filter into vena cava yesterday arvo. That will alleviate risk of clot movement. Right leg moving ok it seems. Facial muscles a bit more expressive today with a smirk/smile at appropriate times. Able to perform peace sign, rock n roll sign and middle finger "up yours" on demand. Awake for longer periods today ... still needs time to build strength tho. Glen is understanding everything we say to her but trachie still in - so not able to speak, swallow, eat, drink or talk. No physio today or tomorrow (weekend?) ... but breathing seems to be good... just needs to get OFF trachie. For those of u asking how I am going ... I had a beer with the boys at the Albion last night (won the meat hamper!) ... and tomorrow going to Optus to watch Eagles beat Richmond courtesy of Mick Pember. Glen's brother John is here from NSW and Dylan, Hannah also on board. Thanks always. We are positive. We feel we are moving ahead". As the army responds I sense they are really on this journey with us as well, clinging on to every little positive. It's a fine line between joy and disappointment. I'm trying hard to paint them a realistic picture but I know some expectations are high.

On Saturday May 12, 2018, the West Coast Eagles defeated Greater Western Sydney in round 8 of the AFL season, followed by a round 9 victory over Richmond. I had never been to a football game at the MCG and, at that point in time those two opponents were the premiership fancies. I took a punt and booked a few tickets for the Grand Final in September. Dylan, Jake, Johnny Luscombe and I flew out on Thursday 27th for the game on Saturday 29th. My brother Gerry managed to score a ticket to the game and couch surfed our apartment in Little Bourke Street. In a dream come true, the Eagles not only made it to the GF against Collingwood, but won the game in the dying seconds by 4 points. We were seated right behind Dom Sheed as he kicked the winning left foot kick for goal. The stadium atmosphere was electric, that game going down as one of the greatest Grand Finals in AFL history. It was certainly the best game of football I have ever seen. Stumbling into Vamos, a Latin American themed restaurant and wine bar the night after, we discovered superb live music and amazing flamenco dancing. I was so taken by the whole experience I wanted to share it all again with Glen. It was on the bucket list.

Crypto remained a fairly minor allocation in our investment portfolio until the bull market of late 2017. Prices went ballistic, and before the crypto winter of 2018 - 2020 set in, we had locked in substantial profits. The foray into self-managing our ASX investments was also tracking nicely as I gained more experience trading. I had time to drill down at a micro level and was enjoying it immensely, before putting all trading on hold in preparation for our holiday. We flew out of Sydney on August 14th 2017, our wedding anniversary. Because we had crossed the international date line, we arrived San Francisco the same day, giving us two 35th wedding anniversaries!

I was disappointed with the downtown city centre. I remembered the city well from my time as a backpacker and it looked tired, grey and bruised. The same old tourist haunts were busy - Fisherman's Wharf, Golden Gate bridge, Sausalito, but I saw a lot of broken dreams, blank faces and homelessness. We took BART to Mission, walked past the endless boarded up graffitied shop fronts, through Dolores Park and up into Noe Valley, searching for the vibrancy on Haight Ashbury. I couldn't find it. All I found was a rambling, spaced out tripper telling me "nice hair man, nice hair" … the irony was, of course, I didn't have much hair. There was an exhibition in the de Young Art Gallery in Golden Gate Park, celebrating 60's art from the social revolution. I thought very seriously about buying a signed Stanley Mouse poster, but settled instead for a cheap Summer of Love '67 cap, I should definitely have bought the poster. San Francisco felt like it was comfortable in its time warp, living out the glory days of the 60's and 70's, but I knew as soon as our tour guide pointed out "the tree that Janis Joplin sat under playing her guitar" that it actually smelt like a time warp. We enjoyed riding electric bicycles across the bridge, catching the ferry past Alcatraz and the Segway rides around Golden Gate Park, but had it not been for the timelessness of Dolores Park, with its meandering pathways and magnificent views across the city, each of my treasured memories may have bled into the abyss of amnesia. We reminisced about how I finally did meet Santana in 2003. Seated at a downstairs bar in the Hyatt Regency Hotel in Perth, having a quiet drink after the Shaman concert, I recognised him, relaxing with a "minder". Glen insisted I overcome my shyness and fear of rejection ... "if you don't go and introduce yourself you will regret it for the rest of your life". I knew immediately she was right. We chatted for about 10 minutes and, when I spoke of his early days busking in Dolores Park he chuckled, "I'm still busking, it's just that the hat is a lot bigger these days". Next morning, our daughter Hannah joined us downstairs for breakfast, and he was gracious enough to again spend time with us as a family. In true hippie style his parting words were memorable ... "never lose your childhood innocence".

Mon 14th June

Hannah drove me to Optus Stadium last night where the Eagles got up by 4 points in a thriller over Richmond, 85 to 81. It's the second-best game of football I've ever seen. It's now 27 days since Glen's first bypass operation. After her "breakthrough" day 4 days ago when she was awake, animated and responsive for a relatively extended period, I'm fearful she may have regressed a little. I'm hoping its just exhaustion from the blood filter op and moving from bed to chair etc. The wonderful medical staff have all told me she will recover in cycles and I know I'm being impatient, but I can't help myself as this roller coaster goes into loop mode. I'm wanting her to be awake all the time.

We took the overnight Starlight Express train from San Francisco through the Rocky Mountains to Vancouver. Canadian border control officers picked up on my deportation in 1977, and took me aside for interrogation. I had previously returned to Canada with my parents in 1980, so didn't see why this visit would be an issue. After a 2 hour delay I was finally permitted entry, only because I remembered the name of the woman who signed my exoneration letter in 1979 – I had kept Doreen Steidle's official letter taped into my number two scrapbook, bless her soul. From the Vancouver waterfront we called Pete, my mate from Hawaiian days, before hopping aboard the Seabus, for the ferry ride across Vancouver Harbour to meet him and his partner Lana, in North Vancouver. It was fantastic to see Pete again and together we explored the usual tourist haunts, but for me, the highlight was undoubtedly just sharing it all with Glen - a suspension bridge to walk amongst the ancient trees in Lynn Canyon, a late-night stroll with wild skunks at Deep Cove, a picnic stopover high above the harbour waters where Pete revealed 2 guitars he had concealed in his car. Kicking off with Neil Youngs' Harvest Moon, we jammed an impromptu concert attracting a small group of total strangers all dancing to the groove. A late dinner at Horseshoe Bay was the piece de resistance, the Vancouver vibe was alive and well.

We'd organised to hire a car for the drive from Vancouver to Jasper. I was keen on a Mustang but Glen was not impressed, even less so when we discovered I'd misplaced my driver's licence and she had to drive. We ended up with a white Toyota Camry. It had beige interior, very beige actually. Jake was working as a cabin cleaner for Alpine

Village, a well-known accommodation destination in Jasper and, having a mechanical background he'd become a handy maintenance guy as well. Popular amongst the permanent staff and other workers, he'd been singing and playing guitar at the local Leagues club. Jasper is all about mountains, ski fields, Lake Maligne, Spirit Island and the Athabasca River - but I will always remember it for playing Flame Trees with my son in the Jasper Leagues club. They had a full stage set up with great sound and lighting, the beers were flowing and, we performed the duet with Glen and the crowd loving it.

One chilly morning while I was still sleeping, Glen was curious enough to investigate some unusual animal noises. Cautiously approaching a small group of people, she noticed a huge belligerent elk in the distance. The elk had pinned a man to the ground and was goring at him with its massive antlers. Glen instinctively turned and sprinted to get help from Jake, the only person she knew in Alpine Village. Breathless by the time she found him in the gym, Jake thought she was having a heart attack as she related the danger. As our backpacker rushed to the rescue, it became Jake the Aussie Saviour versus the Rampant Bull Elk - a fair enough match up to me. I'm still asleep of course. Glen relaxed and slowly walked back toward the action, confident that her Aussie cleaner son somehow knew how to tame the out of control elk. As she strolled closer, the crowd suddenly turned and began surging back past her yelling "run, run, it's coming, it's coming, run"! So again, she's sprinting, really panicking, only this time she opens a random car door and two of them jump in, seeking refuge with a total stranger. I'm still asleep of course.

As I recall our time in Jasper, I'm reminded of the many times Glen and I commented that each day just kept getting better than the day before. One day we were paddling a classic Canadian canoe on crystal clear Lac Beauvert, the next day chugging a few Labatts from the Adirondacks on the banks of the Athabasca River then, hiking the Valley of the 5 Lakes or enjoying the silence of Spirit Island. We visited every postcard memory along Icefields Parkway, hugging the Athabasca and Bow Rivers all the way to Banff. As we passed Athabasca Falls, Lake Louise and the Glacier itself, every turn of every corner was a painting. I never realised until later, when back in Australia, that I'd struck the same poses my father had, when he was photographed on Banff Bridge and the Athabasca Falls in 1945. All this time we had our son Jake by our side. Enjoying these moments together was truly Glen's idea of the perfect holiday - well ok, it was mine too.

Tues 15th June

Today has been a shit day. Our concerns over Glen's slow response progress has aligned with doctors concerns over her increasing heart rate, and they ordered a CT scan last night. The results are back and they are not good. Glen has had another bleed on the right side of her brain. They've stopped and reversed the heparin infusion. Hannah sends out a text: "Just sitting beside Mum, holding her hand while we listen to some old classics... every now and then she taps her fingers along to the music of a particular favourite, like Van Morrison, Paul Simon, Dusty Springfield, Elvis and The Police. Last week we thought we had turned the corner as Mum seemed to have been starting to have more wakeful periods and stronger responses and purposeful movements, but a good 3 days of gradual improvement was followed by the last 3 days of Mum not really opening her eye at all ... and less frequent and weaker responses/movements. Yesterday afternoon, after

Dad expressed some concerns about Mums responsiveness, they did a CT scan and this morning we were told that it showed some new bleeding in her brain. This was always a risk factor of the heparin infusion that was started to prevent the clots in her lung and legs from growing, or any new ones forming, a risk we were praying she would avoid. So now the anti-coagulation has ceased, and with it hopefully the bleeding too. Apparently, the location of the bleed is in the same area that is already damaged, so there is some hope that no new damage has occurred ... but like always no one can say for sure. So, we are praying now that the bleeding has stopped, and that it didn't cause more damage than was already present, that the clots don't grow and that this lapse in wakefulness is just a few rest days while her body was dealing with some additional trauma. One little glimmer of hope this afternoon was, she wiggled her left big toe on request for the nurse... that leg hasn't shown any response for a week now. So, fingers crossed it's coming back and proves responses are not necessarily consistent and can come and go over time.

Our poor Mum is being dealt the most difficult hand... but still she fights, full of grace and with the loving energy of all her (and our) friends and family behind her, lifting her up each day we know eventually she will win". I sit with Glen until 1pm. Overnight, she apparently pulled the nasogastric tube completely out, so they have placed a mitten on her right hand. With nurse permission, I take it off. Glen squeezes my fingers, stroking her thumb against mine. She understands every word we say and she overhears the scan results discussion. We don't want to hide anything from her. At 1pm I left the hospital and drove 230 kilometres straight to Balingup, to collect Glen's remodelled wedding ring. It's beautiful. I pray that tomorrow when I drive back to Perth she's sitting up in bed with 2 eyes open as I slip it on her finger - I know that's unlikely, but none of us know the future and all things are possible. Apart from her time in hospital, Glen's wedding ring has never been off her finger since the day we married. At home in Bunbury a few weeks ago, when life was normal, I'd glanced at our regular shopping list - naked ginger, milk, cauliflower and toothpaste ... and offered to take a quick drive to the supermarket. I chuckled when I saw she had scrawled "Diamond pave ring" at the top of the list. I had no idea what a "pave" ring was. She was joking of course, but I saw it as my golden opportunity to be whimsical. Usually, I am the guy who nonchalantly keeps walking when his wife looks in jewellers' windows, but something inside me said "just do it". So, I did. I bought what turned out to be the diamond pave ring of her dreams. The joy I received, when she discovered the boxed ring as she unpacked the groceries was priceless. We went back to the jeweller and bought matching ear studs. She was worth it, and I realised I had waited far too long to spoil her. Of course, once Glen had the new jewellery, her old ring didn't match at all, so we commissioned to have the old one remodelled, hence my flash trip to Balingup. On the way back to Bunbury I felt the need to drive past my Mum and Dad's old Donnybrook house, the 2-bedroom duplex half where our 3 kids shared their first bedroom, and then the Boulder Street house we built as new. They were both cold and distant now, but for some reason they were calling to me. That night I slept in our Bunbury bed alone, and yes, the indentation of Glen's head was still in her pillow.

Leaving Jake behind in Jasper was bittersweet but, after an amazing time we were booked to fly out of Calgary for New York. One last walk down Patricia Street saw Glen squeal with delight when she found an authentic Lamb Chops soft toy, with "I love you" and "will you play with me" voices, in a gift shop run by a lovely Egyptian/Canadian lady. Straight to the pool room for the grandchildren.

Everything about New York is a movie - Central Park, Times Square, Grand Central Station, Brooklyn Bridge ... everything. For 4 nights and 5 days we got to play the actors. It wasn't enough time, but we managed to squeeze the brass balls on the Wall Street bull, catch the Staten Island ferry past the Statue of Liberty, walk the Highline and Brooklyn Bridge and sweet talk the Bottega Veneta guy on Madison Avenue for a free sample. Glen had taken extra steroids for the NYC holiday leg as she knew the walking would test her rheumatoid arthritis. It turned out to be a sensible precaution, as the day we walked the Highline and got lost in the Chelsea Markets, we covered 26 kilometres.

I cajoled Glen into taking the iconic horse drawn carriage ride through Central Park, past John Lennon's Strawberry Fields and the Bethesda Fountain to Alice in Wonderland. We walked The Mall - 4 rows of towering American Elm trees that form a cathedral like canopy over the park bench where Audrey Hepburn sat in Breakfast at Tiffany's. Every boy I grew up with, fell in love with Audrey Hepburn. I'm sure I could see Meg Ryan in When Harry Met Sally, as we chanced upon the Loeb Boathouse. Bookings weren't accepted but, as we were reading the trading hours, the door flung open and we found ourselves first in line, being escorted to an amazing table overlooking The Lake. The maître d' mistook me for a famous retired New York Yankees baseball player and we enjoyed a lovely chat, before I ordered what was a delicious Nicoise salad with fresh tuna.

Guilty of overacting the classic Central Park love scene, I rented a small boat and rowed Glen toward a bend in The Lake, where a lone saxophonist was busking the approach to famous Bow Bridge. We became voyeurs when, in the boat ahead of us, a young man got down on one knee and started proposing to his girlfriend. We felt a little awkward to be sure, but his excited Dad, running on the bank while filming and cheering, made us chuckle.

No visit to New York is complete without going to a show on Broadway. We were renting on West 42nd street in Hell's Kitchen, not too far from the Stephen Sondheim Theatre, where Carol King's life story production "Beautiful" was showing. Dressed in our sharpest gear, I hailed a yellow cab outside our 414 Apartments. We excitedly jumped into the cab heading for Broadway and sat there, and sat there, and sat there. Traffic was gridlocked and we weren't moving at all. We were now in danger of being locked out in the pre-show opening blackout. We had scoped out the theatre on one of our walks, I knew where it was. Slipping the cab driver $20 we ran, in the rain, Glen barefoot holding her dress up. We made the queue in time to watch a choreographed group of wannabe dancers paying their dues, busking in the adjacent alleyway … the perfect location. Beautiful ... was everything we wanted it to be. We both loved Carol King's music of course, but the sets were fast moving and the plot line fascinating. Seeing the back story behind Tapestry unfold on a Broadway stage was mesmerising. Half way through the show, a lovely American woman sitting next to Glen asked her if she was enjoying the show. In true Julia Roberts style, Glen replied … "it was so good I almost peed my pants"! It was, and she nearly did.

Thurs 17th June

Because the traffic has been horrendous, I arrived at the hospital car park at 9.15am before catching a coffee with

Marg and Kim Lane at la Galette on Hampton Rd. Marg is Johnny Luscombe's elder sister. She has literally motivated a whole congregation to pray for Glen and I appreciate it. I know Marg is worried about me as well as Glen. I assure her I'm fine but, I shed a tear with her anyway. By the time I'm at Glen's bedside it's 10.40am and her heart rate is 143. I freak out and try to grab nurse Bronte's attention, but she's attending to another urgent patient. Glen's left eye is wide open and has a look of distress about it. I take the mitten off Glen's right hand and start running through questions that need a binary answer ... are you in pain? Thumbs up for yes. Is the pain in your head? no. Leg? no. Arm? no. Finally, after every body part I can think of, I say bladder and the thumb goes up immediately. This is strange as she has a catheter fitted but Bronte says she will do an ultrasound check for any issues. Suddenly, there is a code blue in the adjoining room and they ask me to leave HDU. On my return, Bronte tells me Glen's catheter was blocked with sediment and Glen's bladder was emptied of 700 mls. They've sent a urine sample away for testing, flushed and fitted a new catheter and Glen is peacefully sleeping. Her heart rate is 113 at 14 breaths per minute. She's comfortable. I'm so proud of Glen, even semi-conscious Glen's a good nurse, diagnosing her own problems. Rodger tells me she is booked in for an echocardiogram this afternoon. Sushi for lunch, a cup of English Breakfast tea and a quick power nap in the car and I'm back in at 3pm. Glen's heart rate is 95, 13 BPM and 98 oxy ... better.

We flew out of Newark, New Jersey for Las Vegas - to see for ourselves what has to be one of the craziest places on the planet. Glen had booked us into Tuscany Suites on East Flamingo just off Las

Vegas Boulevard, only problem being, she had booked us for exactly one month prior. Luckily, we got a room and headed straight to the Strip, mingling with various Michael Jackson, Bruce Willis and Elvis lookalikes, before catching the Bellagio Fountains show with a crowd scene straight from The Hangover. Unabashed tourists, we marvelled at the sheer plasticity of the whole place - fake Eiffel Tower, fake New York, fake Venice, fake rain and thunder, even fake rain forest bird calls around the pool. We took in a real Ricky Martin concert, before a visit to Fremont Street confirmed my fears that Vegas was so fake it was real, a smoke and mirrors show of epic proportions ... and it could only happen in America.

My driver's licence was long lost, as was my wish to hire a convertible Mustang. Glen drove our new boring beige Toyota hire car 250 kilometres north-east, to Springdale in Utah, gateway to Zion National Park. If you've seen Butch Cassidy and the Sundance Kid you've seen some of Zion Canyon. It's amazing. Google it, go there if they ever ease Covid restrictions, do whatever you have to, it's worth it. We stayed too long at a local restaurant one night and missed the free taxi back to our accommodation. A couple overheard our anxious conversation and offered to give us a ride home, in their Mustang. I hereby attest, four adults can fit very comfortably into a Mustang ... sort of. Two nights in Springdale before we zig zagged our way up Mount Carmel, through the 1.8-kilometre mountain tunnel to Bryce Canyon and on to Kanab. We temporarily lost GPS signal and, while checking Google maps as we exited the tunnel I missed the herd of bison - damn technology.

Always - The Patsy Cline Story. The promo poster leapt at me from the sea of paraphernalia on the wall in the Rocking V cafe in Kanab. I knew nothing about Patsy Cline other than I liked her song Crazy, written by Willie Nelson. We were still buzzing from Beautiful on

Broadway, and the thought of another night like that was a nice warm feeling. We booked two tickets there and then, as the final show of a limited 7-night season was scheduled for that night in the Redstone Theatre, right next door. The old restored theatre was packed, we must have bought the last two tickets and, as we sat down, an old American military veteran, recognising our accents, leaned forward and spoke to Glen. The old guy got a bit emotional when he found out Glen had been nursing in an aged care facility, and her Dad had served in the allied submarines during WW11. At the end of their conversation, the gentle, skinny old guy, dressed in his checked shirt, oversized Levi jeans and cowboy belt and boots, touched me on the shoulder and said "Make sure you look after this girl son, she's one in a million". I said "Yes, I know" … and I did know. From that moment the band started warming up pre-show and, we knew we were in for a very special night. We were in southern Utah, the heart of cowboy country, the home of over 50 western movies starring John Wayne, Clint Eastwood, Paul Newman and Robert Redford amongst others. Surrounded by a house full of cheering locals in checked shirts, listening to two unbelievable fiddle players duelling on stage in a 6-piece band featuring Johnny Cash's ex steel guitar player, I was absolutely gob smacked. Lyndsey Wulfenstein, head of Dance at Brigham Young University played Patsy Cline, and the highly credentialed supporting cast made our night watching Always, simply unforgettable. The show received over one hundred five-star reviews online, proving so popular it was revived for a second season in 2018.

We detoured into Arizona, to convince ourselves images of Horseshoe Bend on the Colorado River hadn't been photo shopped. Natural beauty never ceases to amaze, it doesn't always need to be spectacular, but dangling my legs over the Navajo Sandstone ridge was a humbling experience. In the increasingly digital life we lead, our lives tend to become crowded and busy and, places of raw majesty seem even more beautiful. Glen and I never got to see the vastness of the Valley of the Monuments (I wanted to do a Tom Hanks), but we did experience the magnificence of the Grand Canyon. Is there any place better than this beautiful planet we live on? I'm reminded of some lyrics by Melissa Etheridge - "All the way to Heaven, is Heaven". It's true. We are surrounded by Heaven, it's just that sometimes we don't see it. Our American dream had come to an end, we were booked to fly out of Las Vegas for San Francisco, then Sydney and home to Perth. Every single day was indeed, better than the day before, but before we left, Glen had just enough time to drop a U turn in the middle of Las Vegas Boulevard, right in front of the Bellagio. It would have been a lot cooler in a Mustang.

Fri 18th June

Jake flew in last night from Roy Hill and we're both at Glen's bedside by 10am. I take the mitten off her right hand and as soon as she hears Jake's voice she opens her left eye and smiles. I send this text to Dylan and Hannah: "Jake and I are in with Glen now ... she has been very aware and comfortable the whole time. We've been playing all her favourite songs on the Ue Boom and she's been smiling and tapping her fingers. She has been "awake" since we got here at 10am ... pretty much the whole time. Jake just told her Tegan was going for her 20 weeks scan next week and Glen mouthed the word Wow! And held her thumb up ... it's a good day so far. Physio due any minute. Xx" Maureen and Riley Horrocks arrive for a visit and Glen is quite animated. Maureen comments that she is more awake than their previous visit. I send this text to the kids: "Mums

> *resting after a visit from Maureen and Riley. Her HR is 86 (excellent), BPM 13, Oxy 100. Perfect."* Glen has been awake continuously now for 2 hours, the longest period so far, I'm encouraged. Physio comes sometime between 1-3 and Glen does 10 minutes off the cuff. She gives herself a pat on the back ... well the chest anyway. Pretty happy with Glen's responses today.

After our American adventure, we were looking forward to staying one night in Perth with Hannah and Kade before making our way home. Our excitement went next level when they told us Hannah was pregnant with our first grandchild. Tears flowed freely on both sides as we knew they had been trying for some time. Marley Nell Boucher was born 1st April, 2018. It wasn't too long before Glen started saying "she's very advanced for her age!" We returned home to our Bunbury town house where, as I'm unpacking, I find my "lost" drivers licence ... on the bedside table where I left it. Magic. How it got there from being lost in America is just pure magic, beyond me. The upstairs bathroom renovations were complete, transforming and modernising the area, so we set about redesigning the balcony, downstairs bathroom and a new kitchen. New plantation shutters, floor coverings and lighting, together with a new coat of paint and new furniture throughout gave the whole place a fresh, coastal feel.

In the midst of what seemed like a chaotic episode of House Rules ... Dylan and Karlee surprised us with fantastic news that they too, were expecting a baby! It was difficult to know who was the most excited, them as first-time parents, or us, expecting two grandchildren within 6 weeks of each other. While I was busy converting a downstairs bedroom into my new upgraded STEM music studio, Glen was busy finding the artist within, painting a Positano inspired fresco on a garden wall. Turkish and Moroccan tiles featured in panels against the neighbouring sandstone walls, and a working "Under the Tuscan Sun" rustic wall tap added to the romance. Travertine floor tiles, terracotta potted olive trees and cypress pencil pines, some colourful hanging baskets and a huge pomegranate tree completed the deal ... until Glen decided we needed a small red and white striped awning, to match the one she'd painted in the fresco. Our beach house was finally complete and our private little Mediterranean enclave would soon fill with the sounds of laughter, music and babies. Before that would happen however, Glen had to buy a giant white stork, complete with tiny sheet and baby doll, for Karlee's baby shower. Addison James Trigwell was born 6th June 2018. Within a few short weeks, Glen was telling us she was definitely advanced for her age! It was now time for some guitar and red wine.

Our lives settled in to a comfortable rhythm of babysitting, gardening, cooking, sunsets, coffee and more babysitting. I was back into a morning ritual of checking the ASX for announcements, trading and researching. We knew we had the best neighbours we could ask for and we celebrated for the sake of it, even occasionally resorting to impromptu costumes and karaoke singing into celery sticks. Celery stick microphones add a nice crunch to the voice by the way. The Tuscan tap continued to trickle water into the fish pond and, my first crop of 26 pickled Kalamata olives was a huge success.

Glen's Dec 2018 birthday was getting closer and I recalled my bucket list promise to see the Flamenco dancer and guitarist with her. After confirming a gig date, I secretly booked a table for two at Vamos and told Glen to pack her bags for a mystery destination. The kids knew my plans but Glen had no idea, right up until the moment we boarded our flight to Melbourne. It was such fun. Everything went to plan, the show, meal and drinks were fantastic and Glen was chuffed to meet Aya and Alejandro, dancer and guitarist, after the show. As young adults during Stage 2 of our lives, we never travelled together. Now, 40 years later we were doing it all again as baby boomer backpackers, without the tent. I finally understood my Mum's "golden years", our lives became a carousel of simply enjoying our time together.

We'd bought a Jayco Penguin camper trailer in 2014. We referred to it as our "cubby" and had mostly used it for gold prospecting and camping in remote outback areas. Glen's brother Charlie sparked my interest in metal detecting years earlier, when he loaned me a machine on a camping trip and after two days wandering around the outback bush I found my first ever nugget. Glen bought a special display frame from the Perth Mint, the massive specimen sits suspended, seemingly in mid-air, all 0.5 gram of it. Charlie was experienced, very knowledgeable and had great survival skills. If you're ever going to get lost in the outback, get lost with Charlie. Going bush with Charl and Shirl became a unique experience and a real pleasure, I found a few nuggets but they were always just a bonus really. Wandering in the day time, followed by a few songs around a campfire, a couple of beers or glass of red under a Pilbara night sky and gold stories … they were the real nuggets. We undertook a few road trips to Karijini, Broome, Monkey Mia, Exmouth and Esperance over the years, even travelling to Glen's birthplace Leonora. We made our way to Lake Ballard, past the stark Antony Gormley sculptures, for a family reunion in the ghost town of Mount Ida, Glen's childhood hometown. Her brother John had towed his caravan across from New South Wales to be at the outback get together where Joop and Nell's ashes would finally be laid to rest. Camped under a tall stand of mulga eucalypts, we sat in a circle, surrounding Charlie as he poked, prodded and perfected a camp roast over the open fire. As the afternoon wore on, there were guitars, singing voices, time lapse photography and a few beers, making for a fine and fitting family affair. We all had a laugh at John's expense, when I pressed the remote button on my rock n roll smoke machine, surreptitiously placed under John's caravan earlier in the day. The following day they dug a hole in the red pindan dirt, burying their parents' ashes at the foot of an old and crooked wooden post. Saying a prayer, they sprinkled everlasting flower seeds around the neat front garden gate. I saw an old twisted metal frame on a broken hinge, where the everlastings will bloom forever.

In July 2019, our son in law Kade was involved in a charity, raising money to build schools for children in Cambodia. An auction was held, where one of the main fund raisers, a two-week trip on the True North, never attracted a bid. A small luxury cruise ship, True North was set to cruise the Kimberley coast in North Western Australia within 3 weeks of the auction. Visiting iconic locations such as Prince George River, Mitchell Falls, Montgomery Reef and Horizontal Falls along a wilderness stretch of coastline, we decided to be whimsical again, put in a bid which was accepted and flew to Kununurra. 22 guests boarded from all across Australia and the globe. They were an interesting and diverse bunch, including molecular biologists, advertising executives, health care specialists, a billionaire and Les. Sounds like the theme song from Gilligan's Island doesn't it, which brings me to our billionaire. Only a relatively young man, he stood in the US elections of 2016, meeting and campaigning alongside Donald Trump. His father had built a huge family business around oil interests and property, turning over US$5 billion per annum. He was the property manager and, as I would discover over a few nightcaps, an avid guitar collector. We played a few songs together and chatted about life, resonating over similarities we both faced when business and family collide - I resonated with ten less zeroes. He had another hidden talent though, he'd memorised episodes from old TV shows, such as Gilligan's Island, Green Acres, Beverley Hillbillies and F Troop and could sing the theme songs from every show we threw at him. So, who is Les? Lesley Howson, mother of Craig Howson owner of the True North, and fan of impromptu guitar singing sessions. We struck an onboard friendship with Les and she has been a great support to me while Glen is in hospital. Craig was an early pioneer of trips along the rugged and sometimes unchartered waters of the Kimberley coastline. With superb food and beverage, unique eco experiences and on-board helicopter, we were privileged to discover a rare corner of our wonderful world aboard True North. Mud crabbing, oyster harvests, barramundi fishing and crocodile sightings together with dugong, whale and turtle watching kept us all enthralled, while isolated billabong swimming, heli-fishing, remote waterholes and bush heli-picnics were real outback experiences. Spoilt by Rhys Badcock winner of Master Chef Pro 2013, we indulged in masterpiece dishes, within hours of us catching and collecting magnificent fresh ingredients. I'm reminded of the Eagles lyrics "They called it paradise, I don't know why, you call some place paradise, kiss it goodbye". Don't go there, you'll hate it.

Unexpected Inspiration

Viewing Gwion Gwion Bradshaw figures and Wandjina rock art were highlights of our experience in the Kimberley. It's surreal lying in a cave, on a rock floor looking up at ancient Wandjina art, knowing that the artist lay in that exact same spot perhaps 60,000 years before. The artist is long gone, but the fact his rooftop art lives on … is testament to the power of true expression. Did the artist ever imagine the musing would be so enduring and admired? One minute I was inspired by amazing aboriginal rock art, then in the next minute humbled, standing before an ancient burial cairn where it was impossible, not to share a deep sense of ritual and respect. I finally found words to finish a song I had been sitting on for over 18 months. Autumn Day was a melody, intro and first verse, which I liked lyrically, but was going nowhere musically. A sense of presence at the stone burial site provided the key for a one-line metaphor, unlocking a minor musical shift and the remaining lyrics. I like to think I had some help from a 60,000-year-old artist. Maybe I did? I certainly had help from Alan Payne on grand piano. I finished recording all audio tracks just before Covid hit in March 2020. The final track was a children's choir from Our Lady of the Cape primary school in Dunsborough, recorded in the school auditorium under the direction of Maureen Horrocks. Maureen had been coaching and directing award winning choirs throughout her professional career.

Covid lockdown was spent mixing and mastering in STEM studios, before Autumn Day was released on all major streaming platforms 6th June 2020. I always felt the song was a gift, a chance to express my true self and I'm proud of it.

Gerry asked if we were interested in flying to Alice Springs then renting a car for a drive to Uluru. He planned a week away exploring the red centre visiting Kings Canyon and the MacDonnell Ranges as well as the rock itself. We'd only just disembarked the True North and were already booked for a 3-week tour of Tasmania in late November but jumped at the opportunity. Gerry and his wife Rose were keen to climb Uluru before the traditional owners, the Yankunytjatjara and Pitjantjatjara people closed the climb forever on 26th October 2019. With no desire to climb, Glen and I chose to circumnavigate the rock on foot, about a 10-kilometre walk. We had a strange and beautiful experience as we strolled the base of Uluru. We heard a beautiful, familiar bird call coming from a heavily wooded area. As we investigated the unmistakable song, our "Brownie" flew down and sat on a branch not more than 30 centimetres away from our faces. Brownie was the most amazing grey shrike thrush who visited us every day at the farmhouse after we completed the renovations. About now, most people will think I'm crazy, but throughout my entire life I only ever saw one grey shrike thrush on our farm and Brownie was it. Russ and I were both avid bird watchers and would often watch and count the many bird species we'd seen on the farm. Glen regularly fed the blue wrens, willy wagtails and new holland honeyeaters from our kitchen window but, to my knowledge, no-one had ever seen a grey shrike thrush. One day Brownie just arrived. He hopped straight inside the house like he owned it and just sat there, singing, watching us. Every morning he would welcome the sunrise outside our bedroom window, singing ostentatiously and, when we sat outside for coffee, he would ever so politely sit on the armrest of our chair and sing continuously. One day, Brownie disappeared, forever. We were sad, never quite understanding why we were given such an uplifting magical gift, until Uluru. Brownie sang the same welcome, the same songs, with the same joy, just for us. When he flew down and perched right in front of us, it felt like he had been waiting, all this time, for us to arrive. We visited the Uluru Parks and Wildlife offices enquiring about grey shrike thrush habitat and told them our story. They told us grey shrike thrush were very rarely if ever, sighted at Uluru, difficult to get close to, and impossible to approach. All things are possible. All our dreams are locked in time. As Brownie sang before us again, we felt a reciprocal gift was given us for paying our respects to the traditional owners. Others will disagree and call it coincidence, but it just felt right, and as Tom Hanks says in Radio Flyer, "History is in the eyes of the teller, truth is in how he tells it" ... and I'm telling it.

Sat 19th June

Jake is at the hospital by 10am, Glen has left eye open, squeezes his hand, gives him a crooked smile and a wave when he leaves for Margaret River at about 11.15am. He tells me later that, after communicating with Glen via thumbs up, he is of the opinion she has come a long way since the last time he saw her. I get there at ~11am and Glen seems to be sleeping and relatively unresponsive. I don't push her. In the afternoon Charl and Shirl visit and again, Glen is apparently interacting and communicating. Shirley is quite emotional when she returns to the waiting room and confides that is the first time she has seen any response from Glen. She was beginning to think we had been imagining the improvements noted in my texts. She was doubtful the small signs were really there ... that maybe we wanted them to happen so badly we were imagining them. Only 2 people are allowed in to the room at any one time and, by the time I'm back in Glen is asleep again. I start to doubt myself. Maybe I am imagining a gradual improvement? I so badly want a day where Glen leaps forward ... give me 4-5 hours or even more, off the trachie, eye open the whole time, much more alertness when awake, maybe a strong left leg movement on demand - I'm fearful she may have lost that left leg as it seems to have regressed to nothing again. I'm really searching for a big turnaround and getting impatient again. Am I too close to the tiny everyday improvements to appreciate Glen's overall progress? I know I cannot let any doubt or negative reveal itself, particularly in front of Glen, she is fighting so hard. I leave Hannah with Glen and drive to McNeil Street, for a pizza night with Mick and his boys Joel and Ben. We solve the problems of the world, talk about crypto, universal basic income, racism and cultural differences, concerts we never got to see, concerts we did see. Ben is a fan of early techno pop music, and I learn that a 12" vinyl album I bought as a teenager is now considered a valuable collector's item. Yellow Magic Orchestra out of Japan - I can't even remember why I bought the album, there must have been something on there that I liked? We talk about life, success, failure, the known and the unknown, the six degrees of separation and the circle of life. I dine out on my Santana story one more time, then relate the story of a weird encounter I once had in Bali.

About 10 of us were invited to a group meditation on the rooftop at White Lotus meditation centre in Ubud. Glen was a little nervous, and I had never been in a Kundalini group meditation before, always preferring the solitude of my own mind. Sandeh, owner of White Lotus led the meditation which, after about an hour, culminated in each of us freestyle dancing under the stars. Glen's Mum had not long passed away and Glen had a wonderful experience dancing, when she felt her Mum's arms around her and the tears were streaming down her face in the warm embrace. Sandeh, of Italian descent, became a great friend visiting us twice in Bunbury, one time preparing a grande tavolata in the courtyard for all our family. After the meditation, we all gathered at a small restaurant on Jalan Kajeng and I was seated next to a young woman from South Africa. Her home was Cape Town, a city of around 4 million people. I happened to know just one person in Cape Town, she laughed when I posed the question of course, but as soon as I mentioned my God son Stephen Simm by name, she threw her arms in the air in absolute disbelief. Excitedly, she pulled out her phone, hit contacts and rang him immediately. It turned out she was an actress, Stephen was an author, playwright and well-known script writer. She had worked with him and they were close friends. I'm not sure how that fits in with the six degrees of separation, but it was a weird encounter.

I believe that each of us are the sum total of our life experiences. Sometimes, we get so busy we forget, and our memories shrink to faded photographs and another's narrative. When we sit and share, we all become raconteurs, we all get to share in the richness of each other's lives. Its why we sit around campfires keeping stories alive, it's why we write books, its why we treasure heirlooms. How much have we forgotten? How much have ancient cultures remembered? It's been happening like this for thousands of years, all around the world. Like I said ... life can be joyful, if you want it to be.

Glen's 1976 sojourn through Europe inspired us to reunite part of that kombi dream team. We contacted Phill and Judy, two of the original backpackers and, together with Phill's brother Pete and his wife Jan, six of us toured Tasmania in late November 2019. Exploring the Apple Isle in a couple of hire cars for 3 weeks, with such beautiful people, finding such joy in each other's company and finding so many hidden gems along the way made for an amazing 3 weeks. Nice wines too. We had an awesome time catching wild trout on the Hellyer River, learning about Sarah Island's convict past and marvelling at The Mona and The Wall galleries before, on 4th Dec 2019, aged 66, I made my first ever snow man on Mount Wellington. Never lose your childhood innocence.

Sun 20th June

I wake at 6.38am to the sound of heavy, steady rain. A quick shower, dress and coffee and I take both Glen's new rings into hospital, remove the mitten and slip them on her right hand as the left fingers are too swollen. She twinkles her fingers. Her eyes are both closed but she clenches my hand and rubs her thumb against mine. I text the kids: "They just did Glen's obs ... 131/94 with a HR of 104. Right side responses excellent, poked tongue out repeatedly but nothing on left side today ... just a reflex withdrawal to pain on left leg. No reflex withdrawal of left arm. Eyes closed entire time but pupil response in left eye. I connect the Ue Boom and she's finger tapping away to Gladys Knight and the Pips."

Hannah sends out a text to the Second Division: "I spent this afternoon/evening with Mum ... for some short periods she had her eye wide open and was able to watch a few videos of the kids and see some recent photos, she smiled and also shed a few tears because as much as seeing their faces must bring her joy, I know it is breaking her heart that she hasn't been able to see or hold them in too long now. She was thumbs up and shaking her hand to answer questions, while I tried to get the bottom of her discomfort, which we figured out was a headache and also feeling hot under the rugs. So, it's been good that she is able to communicate a bit better... like Dad deciphering that her bladder was causing her pain the other day and him alerting the nurse, who then checked and found her catheter was blocked and her bladder full. Unfortunately, it must be so frustrating for her as she can't communicate unless someone is asking her and, then it takes so long to get to the right question as it's a process of elimination each time. But we seem to be getting there eventually - most of the time. Mum's strength and coordination of her right/arm and leg seem to be improving a little each day, no movement from the left side at all for a couple of days now - but we know now responses can be transient, as she hadn't moved it for a week and then on Tuesday/Wednesday she was doing some small but purposeful knee bends and foot wiggles - showing off her skills while she was visited by her oldest school friend. Today she spent a lot of the day resting, not feeling great as she has been started on antibiotics for another UTI that have upset her tummy. But also, she probably needed a recovery day as yesterday she had a good day, a big day catching up with Jake after he returned from 10 days away at work. She had her eye open for ages, rubbed her belly to signal to him to tell her how Tegan and the baby are going and when he told her they are going for the 20-weeks scan on Monday, she mouthed 'wow'. So that was pretty amazing and super special. She seems to save her energy/exertion for important moments ... always knowing who for and when to give a sign that she's ok. Like today when my uncle and aunty came to see her and she opened her eye for the first time this afternoon, for my aunty who hasn't seen her awake yet. Then while her brother Charl and I were with her the nurse was checking her responses and asked for her to poke her tongue out, she did it lightning quick and forcefully - I commented saying that was so fast and the strongest tongue control I'd seen so far! Uncle Charlie made a joke/comment - I can't remember what it was but the next thing Mum was poking her tongue in and out 3 or 4 times just to stir him up! We all cracked up laughing. Looking forward to Mum being strong enough for the trachie to be reversed so she can talk again ... and for her to be allowed some more time out of bed in the wheelchair - which apparently has been put on hold until they have the results of an ECHO (heart ultrasound) to rule out any more clots, that's been booked, but keeps getting delayed since Thursday. Thanks again to you all for the messages of support and the love, prayers and energy you're sending Mum's way. We all appreciate it and know that it's working ... we just wish it would work a bit faster. Patience is definitely a virtue".

Dream or Nightmare

Jake returned from the snow fields of Alberta and started working at the Roy Hill iron ore mine in North West Australia as a FIFO, or fly in fly out worker. Western Australia has been a major global supplier of iron ore since the 1960's and the economic benefits have underpinned state and national finances for decades. It's not always easy for FIFO workers to lead healthy social lives when their time is split by rosters and distance, however Jake managed to meet his soul mate online and their relationship was blossoming nicely. Within a year Jake had sold his Bunbury house and moved to Margaret River to be with Tegan.

Taking my own advice "life can be joyful, if you want it to be", I secretly planned a surprise boy's day out for Dec 9th 2020. The Brunswick slot car club had become the oldest continually operating club of its type in the southern hemisphere so, I invited some mates, my brothers and our kids on a mystery bus trip. A few of the guys, myself and my two brothers included, were foundation members from 1965. Reminiscing over a couple of cartons of beer on the bus, some great '60's music and a nostalgia quiz, we arrived at the secret destination and shared a great day reliving our youth, before meeting our partners for a meal at the Rose Hotel in Bunbury. I had two regrets that day. I should have told Eddie, my mate from primary school, foundation member of the slot car club and ex housemate, where we were going, as he still had his original slot car from the mid-sixties and, Rob Wotherspoon, the fastest runner in our school years wasn't there. Every Friday night, as 12 and 13-year-old kids, we would excitedly dress for slot cars in our coolest gear. I'd wear my brown corduroy shoes, corduroy trousers and corduroy long sleeve shirt. Rob made us all jealous with his full-length lime green crimplene frock coat, featuring high collar, orange embroidery and button up front. When he wore it with the cravat, it was straight from Carnaby Street and off a Rolling Stones album cover. Unfortunately, nowadays Rob lives in Perth, suffers from advanced Parkinson's disease and is relatively housebound, making the trip that day too difficult.

Hannah and Kade, meanwhile, had surprised us with the news that they were expecting another child. Our babysitting excursions to Perth became a little more frequent when Lennon Sol Boucher was born 1st November 2020, weighing in at 3,480 grams, a little brother for Marley.

From day one Jake and Tegan were a perfect match and set about organising their wedding day for February 6th 2021. Things were progressing well until the State Government declared a Covid lockdown and State regional borders were implemented, meaning half the wedding party couldn't attend. Jake and Tegan took a gamble that the lockdown would not be extended and rescheduled for 8 days later, Valentine's Day. On the original day of their wedding, an arsonist set fire to the Yallingup bush, their reception centre was evacuated as the inferno threatened the wedding venue and later, the area became a quagmire as heavy rain fell all weekend. Feb 6th would have been a disaster, however Valentine's Day proved a master stroke as the lockdown was lifted, the weather was superb and the wedding was everything they wanted it to be. Glen was in her element, surrounded by family in an extended stay at a resort on Geographe Bay while Hannah and Kade, being keen to settle in Dunsborough, made an offer on a block of land. In the last week of February 2021, Dylan and Karlee confided they were expecting a second child, a sibling for Addi, due in November 2021. They wanted to keep their news under wraps as it was still very early days in the pregnancy. We were over the moon but told no-one.

Some friends of ours had recently bought the Northampton caravan park, about 460 kilometres north of Perth. We decided to hitch up our Jayco cubby and visit them, planning a two week break visiting Geraldton, Horrocks Beach, Pink Lake and the town of Kalbarri. We enjoyed a fantastic time playing tourists in our home State, exploring the gorges of the Murchison River and photographing spectacular sunsets across Chinaman's Beach in Kalbarri. I'd packed the metal detector for a quick jaunt into the Yalgoo area on our way home but, the forecast was for 41c degree heat and, with limited mobile phone coverage at "The Gateway to the Outback", we decided to head back to Bunbury. We knew Hannah had booked us as babysitters on March 27th. On our return from Kalbarri, Jake and Tegan presented us with a small wooden box, inside were a tiny pair of RM Williams boots - they too were also expecting a baby! We knew they were in a hurry to start a family, and the prospect of having two new grandchildren, both due around the same time in November was exciting. Hannah and Kade's plans for moving to Dunsborough were progressing quickly, the offer on the block had been accepted, Kade's south west business interest was gaining significant traction and they were looking at house designs. As grandparents, we were excited to think our 3 children and their families would all be living fairly close by, in our magic part of the world.

After months of indecision, we decided to finally sell the Jayco camper trailer. I spent a few days cleaning it up before Glen advertised it on Gumtree. After 7 years of fun we sold the cubby within a week, to the first person to view it, for $500 more than we had paid. We were genuinely sad to see it go, but something was telling us the time was right.

For some unknown reason Glen began to clean the house like a woman possessed, then proceeded to toss out old clothes, boots, shoes and old outfits. Lastly, she bought birthday presents for Marley and Addi, labelling each gift with their respective name, exclaiming proudly "look how organised I am, now you won't have any trouble finding their presents"! My look of bewilderment caused her to wonder why? ... we never really knew why until later. On March 24th, Glen had a headache in the evening and she took two Panadol just before bed. We'd already packed for a two-night babysitting stay at Hannah's. Waking early on the 25th, she still had the dull pain but offered to drive to Perth while I did a few ASX trades on my mobile phone. As always, Marley was excited to see her Grandma, playing dress ups and keeping both of us preoccupied. By about 5 o'clock I could see Glen was really struggling, trying to disguise her pain from Marley. I went to the kitchen and asked Hannah to take a look at her Mum. Hannah's trained nurses eye noticed one pupil more dilated than the other so I wasted no time in driving her straight to Sir Charles Gairdner Hospital, Emergency Department for assessment.

From that moment forward our lives have never been the same. In an instant, our world changed and we could never go back. We found ourselves swirling in a huge dark sea of uncertainty, everything we thought was normal, suddenly wasn't. The Emergency Department at Sir Charles Gairdner Hospital was incredible, within 5 minutes she was being assessed by a doctor. Everything, suddenly, was out of our control. Already, as the wheels of medical science spun around me, I knew I had to trust these professionals to fix Glen's problem. Within hours, she had been scanned multiple times, referred for base line eye data checks, analysed, admitted and prepped for surgery the very next day. Glen was diagnosed with an inoperable "giant" brain aneurysm 25mm in diameter, behind her right eye. It had been there for a long time, so long it had worn the bone surrounding the eye socket. It was deemed too deep and dangerous for open brain surgery. Gradually, some things began to fall into place. I recalled previous headaches Glen had successfully treated with just Panadol, her trip to the optometrist and subsequent referral to a Bunbury ophthalmologist - a scan was never ordered, they told her it was most likely age related. Glen always had a high pain threshold often dismissing her discomfort as temporary, and most of the time, it was. Panadol always seemed to do the job. It used to worry me though when, before she fell asleep at night, occasionally she would say "just in case I don't wake up in the morning I want you to know I love you". I would always say "don't be silly, you'll be ok", and she was. Just not this time.

Dr Albert Chiu, Clinical Associate Professor, and Interventional Neuroradiologist Consultant at Sir Charles Gairdner Hospital offered a surgical solution - not without risk, but an operation performed regularly with a global success rate of about 90%. The theory was, that after the operation and over time, the aneurysm would shrink and be reabsorbed by the body, thereby relieving pressure and any further danger. It could take weeks or even months, but life would return to normal. Glen was grateful to still be alive and, after a family meeting, agreed to the operation. They wheeled a terrified Glen into the operating theatre within 24 hours of presenting at the Emergency Department with a headache.

On March 26th 2021, Dr Chiu performed the operation. A stent was fed into a vein in Glen's right wrist and chased up through her arm into the right carotid artery, where it was positioned to block any blood flow to the aneurysm. It was late on a Friday night, and we were all at Hannah and Kade's house when we received the call, from an unknown number. The procedure had gone well and was deemed a success. The relief was like a balloon being popped. Everyone instantly burst into tears. We had our Glen back. We sat outside on the front lawn, away from the young sleeping Mums with babies, and drank beer. I knocked off half a bottle of Sailor Jerry rum ... not a good idea. The operation recovery process was incredibly traumatic for Glen. The neurological team had warned there would be an immediate "honeymoon" period post operation, followed by worsening pain 3-5 days after the op. What they didn't tell us, was that the risk of stroke was elevated in the days immediately following the op. My heart sank when I received a call from Glen about 1am the next night. She sounded like she was dying, weeping in agony, her voice hardly audible. In all our time together, I had never heard her in such unbearable pain. It was out of visiting hours but I asked did she want me there at the hospital? She answered yes. I hung up and drove. On arriving at SCGH I found she had been moved from High Dependency Unit to a general ward with 4 beds in the room. I thought she was going to die right there and then. So did she. Her head was exploding with pain they couldn't control, drugs like oxycodone, endone and fentanyl were not working. Ultimately, she was on morphine-based painkillers that proved totally ineffective. Later, describing the pain at a 15, she told the neuro team they needed a new pain scale. "Yes, we know all about that pain, we call it the Suicide Pain".

Eventually, Glen was discharged and we returned to our home in Bunbury with enough prescription drugs to get us thrown in jail. It didn't matter, she had survived and was on the way back. Glen found calmness in her daily meditations and every night we sat, found love and our place in the Universe.

Life was back to normal ... or so we thought.

It was the 17th April 2021.

I began writing.

Stephen Trigwell

EPILOGUE

Wed 23rd June

Showing signs of stabilisation, Glen was transferred to Ward G52 room 6. The physios and speech pathologist began working hard to get Glen off the tracheotomy, preparing her for eventual transfer to Fiona Stanley General Hospital and intensive rehabilitation. From midnight 28th June, the WA State Government declared a 4-day Covid lockdown with no hospital visitors allowed. During this lockdown the tracheotomy was reversed. Using Glen's phone, the nurses called me at 2.35pm and Hannah and I chatted with Glen for 12 minutes. Her voice was clearly audible, faltering and tired, but slow and deliberate. It was like a miracle to hear her voice again, tears were flowing freely, but we were angry we couldn't be there to hold her, support her and cheer her on. When the lockdown was further extended to Tuesday 6th July, I drove to Bunbury Saturday 3rd, for a couple of days respite and to get a few jobs done around our home. As I pulled into the garage I got another 13-minute phone call from Glen. The nurses made the call. She's very flat on the phone, pleading why can't I visit her? I can feel her pain. I know she is feeling really low. She must feel like we have all deserted her. For the first time in weeks she can communicate and there's no one there to listen. I feel like a bastard. I take a video of her Grandma's wind up dancing ballerina, collect a few things, her Dad's walking stick, some Maisie children's books and photos.

Self-isolating in Bunbury, I vacuum the house, wash and polish the car, do a load of washing and hang it out. It rains, and I end up throwing the clothes in the dryer. Our neighbour Anna insists she cooks me a fabulous roast lamb and veggies for dinner and Pete delivers it at 6.15pm. I sleep alone in our bed, it's just not the same. Thunder and lightning crash through the night then I'm awake, packed, showered and dressed, ready for coffee with Beau and Vicki, our other neighbours. Beau proudly shows the wheelchair he bought in preparation for Glen's homecoming. He tells me it retails for $1500, but he got it for a bargain! It looks brand new, customisable, turn on the spot and importantly, only 57cm wide, narrow enough to fit easily through any of our doors. Our other neighbour Pam texts, she used to work with Glen and, as well as being a great celery stick vocalist, she's looking forward to helping and supporting her. We have the most amazing, caring neighbours, I can't wait to get Glen home to Bunbury, her castle will become a refuge of comfort, safety and enjoyment.

Tues 6th July

After 8 days the lockdown is lifted and Jake is first to see Glen at 8.30am. She's talking softly but clearly. I arrive about 9.30am and it is so good to wrap my arms around her. Glen confides she has set up an appointment with a psychiatrist, as she "doesn't want to become a bitter and twisted old woman". Apparently in conversation with a Doctor he commented "you sound angry", she agreed and volunteered the appointment. I'm encouraged, and take this as a logical and rational decision on her part. Hannah arrives with Marley and her first visit to see Grandma is eventful, with Glen being put through a vigorous physio session in the gym. We are all clapping as she completes a series of stretching, reaching and co-ordination tasks, including greatly assisted standing and neck movements. After a 1-hour session she grows weary and they wheel her back to the room. To our surprise, all Glen's personal belongings are on the bed, she is being transferred to Ward G66, Room 4D. The room is familiar, 4D being the same bed she left when transferred for her very first bypass operation.

After being allowed in for the first time in 8 days, we all agree Glen has come a long way, but at the same time we also agree something is not quite right. It's hard to put our finger on it and we're conscious of the fact rehab is still in very early days, but each of us senses a slight change in the way Glen is interacting. She is definitely showing evidence of confusion and maybe irrationality, which may be normal under these circumstances however, it is a bit of a worry to us. Glen mentioned to Jake that she wanted to book 2 flights to Exmouth for our wedding anniversary in 4 weeks time, this is clearly not possible however she doesn't seem able to process that. Her vision in the left eye has deteriorated substantially in all of our opinions. Glen was unable to recognise a fairly large picture of her mother, and couldn't recognise the dress Marley was wearing. As I searched for a tube of cream to rub into her hands, Glen said "it's in my other hand". When clearly it wasn't, I said "no it isn't Glen" and she twinkled her right fingers and said "yes here it is".

At Glen's request, I contact her best friend Steph on her mobile phone and they talk for 40 minutes. Glen's conversation skills are encouraging and I'm sure Steph is impressed but I'm listening, thinking the tone all sounds a little robotic. Glen's voice is soft and slow, to be expected, with glimpses of good and original humour but at the same time expressionless and flat in its delivery. Glen obviously knows her voice is softer as she jokes about how everyone used to comment on her loud voice. I have to cut the call off as Glen grows weary. Of course, she has every reason to be flat and, in her words "pissed off", we all hope in time this will be just a phase. Is this phase 2 of the 5 stages of grief? denial, anger, bargaining, depression and finally acceptance? Maybe, but in the next breath her attitude is positive and determined. This will be hard, but I have no doubt she will do this, she is so strong willed. Superwoman. Do the five stages of grief extend to us as well?

Scott allows me to stay until 9pm. Just before leaving, they do Glen's obs and her heart rate is 114. From my limited medical apprenticeship since 18th May, with Glen on beta blockers this HR is too high. Doctor Amy has previously told me a high heart rate like that is ultimately unsustainable. Doctor Hamish had earlier today told me the results of the echocardiogram from June 22nd were good, no damage to the heart so that was a relief and encouraging. He confirmed what Glen had told me earlier, Prof Lind had visited and they were preparing for a cranioplasty on Tuesday 13th July. The operation involves reinserting the section of skull bone taken out during the decompression craniectomy. Another major op involving another general anaesthetic. Normally this would be a sign of natural progress but I can't help feeling some anxiety about Glen's mental state. Something is just not quite right. Is this apparent confusion the "loss of abstract thinking" Doctor Brad had warned us of on 25th May back in ICU? Glen told me today she was unable to sleep at all last night, and after a big physio session in the gym, maybe she is just tired? I hope so. I remind myself that 2 weeks ago I would have been elated she couldn't sleep. The roller coaster continues.

Wed 7th July

Jake and I are both in Ward 66 at 9.30am. Glen's awake and I ask how she slept ... "not very good, the nurse said I woke at 2am, and I haven't been back to sleep since". Later, I ask the nurse the same question and nurse Stephanie tells me she had a good night's rest ... hmm. Glen is keen to tell us her niece Kimmie was on the ward last night doing her rounds. Kimmie is a pharmacist, but she doesn't work at SCGH, never has, and wasn't working there last night. Glen says "she has worked here for 8 years", but I know she hasn't. This confusion is distressing for us to hear, but we are praying it's temporary and can be resolved with time and rehab. At 1.15pm Jake and I chat with Dr Sook explaining all our concerns. She explains that what we are describing is not unusual and these symptoms may improve in time. Unfortunately, she also explains things like "planning" fall into the abstract thinking category, and Glen may or may not be revealing some deficit in that area. Dr Sook says it really is too early to assess at this stage and, after FSGH rehab, a much clearer picture will emerge.

At 3.17pm, after several days of desperately trying, Glen has a breakthrough, passing urine naturally. I immediately text the kids: "Mum just did a 450 ml wee all on her own ... with no need for a catheter!!!!!!!!" It may not sound like much to a "normal" person but this is a huge step forward for Glen. Dylan's response sums up all our feelings: "You GO MUM!!!!! This is the part where you start showing everyone what miracles are made of!!!!!"

Glen is obviously chuffed and the crooked smile is big. Charlie and Shirl pay a short visit and Glen is alive and forthcoming in talking to her brother. They haven't heard her speak since the trachie was removed. Glen posts another big win for the day, passing urine a second time before becoming fairly restless, complaining of "all over pain" and an inability to sleep. She asks me "how do I normally sleep?" I say "usually on your left side, with my arm around you". We try it ... as I rest my head next to hers on the pillow, her shuffling and restlessness slowly ceases. I send this text to the kids at 7.55pm. "Just leaving Glen now ... she is in a deep sleep, something she has been saying she is not getting. The nurse came in and did an ECG and Glen never moved a muscle. Totally relaxed. She's had a big day ... awake all day, physio, Charl and Shirley were impressed, plus, the good news of not one but TWO normal self-initiated big bladder functions. I think the second one was after you left Jake".

As I'm driving to Hannah's house, I start thinking of all the things we take for granted. Glen's attitude and tenacity for the struggle reinvigorate me to start the process of finishing a couple of songs I'm working on. On arrival I text Alan Payne: "Payney are you at all interested in laying down some keyboard tracks on some songs I'm messing with? Not sure if they will ever go anywhere tbh, just feeling like I need to make an effort to complete unfinished work. No pressure if you are too busy or not in the mood. Totally understandable." He responds: "Forward some files Steve and I'll check them out. Lots of love to all. Al" He's a busy guy I know, but with absolute golden fingers on the keyboard. I feel like I have one chance here. I need to really get my act together and lift my game, I haven't done anything since Autumn Day.

Thurs 8th July

I'm in G66 at 10am and Glen is being showered. As they hoist her into the bed I notice she looks fresh but totally exhausted. She tells me she didn't sleep well, her eyes are red, and Doctor Amy queries me on her "confusion episodes". I know the medical team are concerned about her mental state, from both a psychological and potential brain damage point of view. Doctor Amy reassures me that the surgeons will not be touching the actual brain during the cranioplasty, and they wouldn't be scheduling the operation unless Glen was ready for it. The head and lung scans have been brought forward to today sometime. Rodger from HDU pops in to check on Glen's progress. He should have won ICU Nurse (the reality show), only he was ineligible because he works in HDU. Hannah brings Lennon in about 11.15am but Glen is asleep, upon awakening she doesn't recognise Hannah at the end of the bed. Her voice is familiar though, and Glen quickly engages in a lively exchange, asking questions of a general nature. Only time will tell if Glen has any deficit in her so called "abstract thinking" capabilities.

Prof Lind and Doctor Dorian arrive and after a lengthy conversation with Glen, we get to speak privately in the corridor. Prof Lind suspects Glen may be suffering from Syndrome of the Trephined, commonly known as sinking skin flap syndrome. The area where Glen's skull bone was taken out has now taken on a very concave, sunken appearance and could explain some of her recent worrying symptoms. It is a serious condition associated with sensorimotor deficit and neurological deterioration following decompressive craniectomy. Encouragingly, it's possible early cranioplasty intervention can lead to a remarkable clinical recovery, with improvement in the cognitive behaviour and motor deficit, with a rapid reversal of the sensorimotor paresis, reflecting an improvement in brain perfusion. Basically, if Prof Chris Lind is correct, this offers us a real ray of hope for improvement. In the meantime, we're praying she doesn't deteriorate any more between now and Tuesday. While we are chatting, Glen manages another 450 ml wee, without the catheter. Wow, that's 2 yesterday, 2 last night and now one this morning already. The bladder is back! At 5.28pm they wheel Glen out for the scans. Hannah thinks Doctor Amy and Doctor Sook have taken note of our post lockdown observations, prompting the bedside visit by Prof Lind and the scheduled early cranioplasty.

Fri 9th July

9.45am Glen has been in physio for 30 minutes. She looks totally exhausted. Back at the ward I massage her neck with Fisiocrem and apply a heat pack. I'm worried she appears to be getting worse, constantly fatigued. Dr Shanti told me the scan showed the lung clot has disappeared. Great news. Glen has a cough though, Ashanti's concerned they may have to delay op on Tuesday, so taking bloods today for infection testing. No temperature apparently. Glen falls asleep as nurse Ivy prepares her for the chest X ray. I take the opportunity to head off early for a beer with the boys at the Subiaco Hotel. The good news about Glen's now non-existent lung clot has the army on fire. I get this text reply from Janet: "Hi Steve. Thank you again for the updates. Much appreciated. That's great about the clots. Hope tomorrow's scan news also good. I had a msg from Lynne Lee, via Joan, to ask me to let you and Glen know that there are prayers being said for Glen in Paris, Philippines, Sydney and Melbourne. Sending positive thoughts and love to you all. Special hug for my very special friend"

Sat 10th July

Dylan drives up from Bunbury and he's in first at 9.20am. Dylan is a fantastic positive influence for Glen. I walk past the nurse station at 10.23am and talk to Doctor Amy, Glen's chest X ray from last night shows nothing of concern. This is fantastic. Apparently, her HR is elevated, average 114 overnight. Amy suspects this may be related to the UTI, but it could be Syndrome of the Trephine. They are putting

Glen on a powerful antibiotic, Ciprofloxacin. At 7.55pm we are just about to leave when Glen whispers "I heard the lady in the next bed say, "I wish my Mum was here" ... then Glen, with tears welling in her eyes said, "I wish my Mum was here". It broke our hearts. I could only give her a hug. There was nothing I could say.

At the beginning of this nightmare, in what seems a lifetime ago, March 26th 2021, surgeons positioned a stent inside the carotid artery on the right side of Glen's head. A subsequent scan revealed the stent had failed to stop blood flow to a gigantic aneurysm. Contrary to expectation, the aneurysm actually grew from 25mm to 33mm diameter over a six-week period. A carotid artery bypass operation was performed using a vein from Glen's left arm. The operation was in two parts; a high flow and a low flow bypass. The low flow was a success, however the high flow failed. A second, high flow bypass was performed, this time using a vein from her right leg. It too, failed. Glen suffered a stroke right then. While still in ICU, inter cranial head pressures necessitated a decompression craniectomy, whereby a section of the skull was removed to allow the brain to expand into the space. A subsequent tracheotomy and inferior vena cava filter insertion were followed by the eventual reversal of the tracheotomy.

We think the final step in putting our Humpty back together again is replacing Glen's skull section, in a procedure known as a cranioplasty. We could be wrong. They wheeled Glen in for the operation on Tuesday 13th July 2021 at 3.16pm. She was calm. She waved me goodbye as I took a photo, then drove back to Hannah's house. I hated taking that photo but it had to be taken. Is this the last photo I ever take of Glen? 5.50pm I get a call from Prof Lind on the unknown number. Everything went well. Glen is already awake and talking in the recovery room. I post a text on the family chat: "Just had the call from Chris Lind on the unknown number. The operation went well! Mum will be back in HDU recovery very soon. They also put a temporary Cerebrospinal fluid (CSF) drain in, hoping to wean her off within a week. Yahoo ... a worthy champion" I drive immediately to HDU at SCGH but Glen isn't out of recovery yet. I wait. As the night wears on, I'm growing more and more anxious when twice the nurses tell me they are trying to get Glen's pain management under control. Finally, at 11.02pm, Glen is wheeled into HDU. I text "I'm in with her now, she told me to tell you all how much she loves you. She's holding a very decent conversation and says the pain has definitely subsided since before. Looking a bit sleepy, that's good." The nurses kick me out at 11.22pm.

I could go on recording every detail, every step along the way but, I realise it's a never- ending journey. There will always be another hurdle, another challenge, another fear. This story is not a linear plot where Glen regains all deficits, life returns to our old "normal" and everyone lives happily ever after. Maybe it will turn out that way, who knows? The reality is, regardless, all our lives have been changed forever. Our new normal will be different, but life will still be joyful, because we want it to be. We still have many challenges to overcome, all of us, including medical, mental and rehabilitation issues. Glen's resolve however, in undertaking each challenge with confidence, dignity, pride and always with the expectation of success, will see her win. We don't know how all this will end, except that she and we, will win. There really is no such thing as winning and losing though, we just get to hold this beautiful prize for as long as we can. What I have learnt, is that we don't have to do this alone. The support we have received as a family has been monumental. Our army became armies across continents, and every phone call, gift, card and text of support gave us strength. During the darkest of times we all camped, downhill with our backs to the river. We triumphed in battle, and we will continue to triumph no matter the adversity. For that, we as a family cannot thank our supporters enough.

In all this time, our Champion never once fell from her horse.

Maybe ... just like Chauncey, we will all, nonchalantly stroll out across the surface of a lake.

The End

Stephen Trigwell

Acknowledgment

The whole intent of this story was to fill the gaps of lost consciousness for my beautiful wife Glen. I must thank our children, Hannah, Dylan and Jacob, and their equally amazing partners Kade, Karlee and Tegan. Our lives have been turned upside down and inside out. Only love has held us together, but what more does anybody need? Neil Young wrote ... "one of these days, I'm going to sit down and write a long letter, to all the good friends I've known". This book is my long letter ... to our children and grandchildren, relatives, many friends, the magnificent miracle workers at Sir Charles Gairdner Hospital and all the people who prayed for Glen. I want our army of dreamers and carers to link hands, realise their strength, and remember this time as a testament to their power of love, belief and conviction. Make no mistake, this journey would not have been possible without the unstoppable combined energy we as a family, gratefully accepted.

Stephen Trigwell

www.ingramcontent.com/pod-product-compliance
Lightning Source LLC
Chambersburg PA
CBHW051941290426
44110CB00015B/2067